Veracity of Data

From Truth Discovery Computation Algorithms to
Models of Misinformation Dynamics

Synthesis Lectures on Data Management

Editor
Z. Meral Özsoyoğlu, *Case Western Reserve University*

Synthesis Lectures on Data Management is edited by Meral Özsoyoğlu of Case Western Reserve University. The series publishes 80- to 150-page publications on topics pertaining to data management. Topics include query languages, database system architectures, transaction management, data warehousing, XML and databases, data stream systems, wide scale data distribution, multimedia data management, data mining, and related subjects.

Veracity of Data: From Truth Discovery Computation Algorithms to Models of Misinformation Dynamics
Laure Berti-Équille and Javier Borge-Holthoefer
2015

Datalog and Logic Databases
Sergio Greco and Cristina Molinaro
2015

Big Data Integration
Xin Luna Dong and Divesh Srivastava
2015

Instant Recovery with Write-Ahead Logging: Page Repair, System Restart, and Media Restore
Goetz Graefe, Wey Guy, and Caetano Sauer
2014

Similarity Joins in Relational Database Systems
Nikolaus Augsten and Michael H. Böhlen
2013

Information and Influence Propagation in Social Networks
Wei Chen, Laks V.S. Lakshmanan, and Carlos Castillo
2013

Keyword Search in Databases
Jeffrey Xu Yu, Lu Qin, and Lijun Chang
2009

Veracity of Data: From Truth Discovery Computation Algorithms to Models of Misinformation Dynamics
Laure Berti-Équille and Javier Borge-Holthoefer

ISBN: 978-3-031-00727-9   paperback
ISBN: 978-3-031-01855-8   ebook

DOI 10.1007/978-3-031-01855-8

A Publication in the Springer series
SYNTHESIS LECTURES ON DATA MANAGEMENT

Lecture #42
Series Editor: Z. Meral Özsoyoğlu, *Case Western Reserve University*
Founding Editor: M. Tamer Özsu, *University of Waterloo*
Series ISSN
Print 2153-5418   Electronic 2153-5426

Veracity of Data

From Truth Discovery Computation Algorithms to Models of Misinformation Dynamics

Laure Berti-Équille and Javier Borge-Holthoefer

Qatar Computing Research Institute
Hamad Bin Khalifa University

SYNTHESIS LECTURES ON DATA MANAGEMENT #42

ABSTRACT

On the Web, a massive amount of user-generated content is available through various channels (e.g., texts, tweets, Web tables, databases, multimedia-sharing platforms, etc.). Conflicting information, rumors, erroneous and fake content can be easily spread across multiple sources, making it hard to distinguish between what is true and what is not. This book gives an overview of fundamental issues and recent contributions for ascertaining the veracity of data in the era of Big Data. The text is organized into six chapters, focusing on structured data extracted from texts. Chapter 1 introduces the problem of ascertaining the veracity of data in a multi-source and evolving context. Issues related to information extraction are presented in Chapter 2. Current truth discovery computation algorithms are presented in details in Chapter 3. It is followed by practical techniques for evaluating data source reputation and authoritativeness in Chapter 4. The theoretical foundations and various approaches for modeling diffusion phenomenon of misinformation spreading in networked systems are studied in Chapter 5. Finally, truth discovery computation from extracted data in a dynamic context of misinformation propagation raises interesting challenges that are explored in Chapter 6. This text is intended for a seminar course at the graduate level. It is also to serve as a useful resource for researchers and practitioners who are interested in the study of fact-checking, truth discovery, or rumor spreading.

KEYWORDS

information extraction, truth discovery, data veracity, trust computation, misinformation dynamics

Contents

C H A P T E R   1

Introduction to Data Veracity

1.1   THE FOURTH "V" OF BIG DATA

The maturity of database and Web technologies has encouraged users to make information publicly available in large quantities and various formats, opening up the possibility of large-scale searches and comparative analyses over multi-source data. However, such analyses are difficult due to practical issues in extracting data from textual and multimedia content and integrating data from sources with highly heterogeneous structures, semantics, and qualities. One of the fundamental difficulties is that extracted information can be biased, noisy, outdated, incorrect, misleading and thus unreliable. To add to the problem, available data sources can provide conflicting information, leaving the users with a stack of problems and open questions related to the following.

- *Source selection:* Different information sources may answer a query with different values, response times, query costs, and various degrees of data quality [Rekatsinas et al., 2014, Salloum et al., 2013] and trustworthiness [Bertino et al., 2009, Dai et al., 2008]. Hence, can we define and automate strategies for selecting timely and adaptively the most appropriate sources for query-answering and decision-making?

- *Data quality:* Data quality is a multidimensional concept combining consistency, freshness, completeness, and accuracy of the data as a non-exhaustive list of dimensions to characterize *data fitness-of-use* [Batini and Scannapieco, 2006, Berti-Equille, 2007a,b, Fan and Geerts, 2012, Zaveri et al., 2014]. This context is comparable to a "data market" where multiple providers offer data required by a consumer, but in different ways, through different services, and with various evolving degrees of quality and trust. The user must compare and balance the objective features of each data provider, e.g., cost of access, speed of access, reliability, accuracy, etc. One of the important means of distinguishing between multiple data providers and data sources in such a "data market" is the quality of the data provided. For instance, users may be prepared to pay more for access to data when they are confident that the data is both correct and complete, or they may be prepared to sacrifice (say) the currency of the data if it costs less. Hence, how can we evaluate the quality of the data with objective measures? How can we make value-for-money decisions about which data provider to contract with and which corrective actions to set up over the data and make the best usage of the data even when their quality is not the best?

- *Information provenance:* Provenance metadata captures the manipulation and transformation history of the data starting from its original information source [Hartig, 2009]. From this metadata, one can ascertain data quality from the origin data and derivations, keep the information extraction processing history, and trace errors from their sources. Unfortunately, provenance metadata is often missing and there is no guarantee that a data provider is actually the original source of the data. How do we figure out which is the original data source among a set of providers that provide the same data value without its original context?

- *Data velocity and dynamics:* The real world evolves, data change from one provider to another, and information mutates more quickly than we can ever acknowledge. Conflicting data can be easily spread across multiple sources, making it hard to distinguish between what is true and what is not. How do we figure out that a lie has been told often enough that it is now considered to be true? How many lying sources are required to introduce confusion in what you knew before to be the truth?

With the advent of Big Data, data quality and trustworthiness have become more important than ever. Typically, *volume*, *velocity*, and *variety* are commonly used to characterize the salient features of Big Data. However, the importance of the fourth "V" of Big Data, *veracity* is being more and more recognized [Berti-Equille and Borge-Holthoefer, 2015, Saha and Srivastava, 2014]. In the Database community, *veracity* refers to several quality dimensions related to repairing data inconsistencies and fixing other data quality problems such as duplicates, missing or incomplete data. However, the problem of estimating data veracity should be projected into a bigger picture where misinformation dynamics is modeled and understood. Given the complexity of the truth discovery problem, an interdisciplinary approach is needed.

The focus of this book is precisely to review related work from various research domains in information extraction, fact-checking, trust management, and modeling of misinformation dynamics as presented in Figure 1.1. As illustrated, information providers generate content, and ratings and are organized in evolving networks. This content can be extracted, structured, and formatted as claims that are grouped when they refer to the same real-world entity or event. Fact-checking typically consists of labeling each claim as true or false. Knowledge base population consists of extracting values from a collection of texts and unstructured claims to populate a knowledge base. Trust management consists of computing trust degrees of information sources or providers from referees' ratings and past experiences. Information dynamics studies consist of modeling information propagation in the complex networks of content providers.

1.2   MAIN CAUSES AFFECTING DATA VERACITY

Data quality problems can affect the veracity of data. From a technical perspective, they have various causes along the truth discovery pipeline represented in Figure 1.1 including the following.

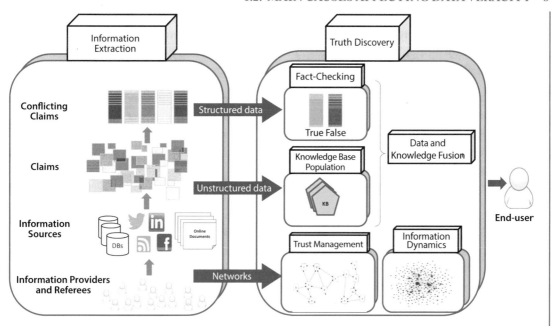

Figure 1.1: Truth discovery pipeline. Various research domains have contributed to the field of Truth Discovery in relative isolation: information extraction with entity linking and slot filling tasks for knowledge base population, fact-checking and data fusion of structured data, trust computation and management in reputation-based and recommender systems, and information dynamics in complex networks. This book will survey the different contributions to the problem of truth discovery.

- Limits of data collection and data sensing: Technical equipment can have measurement errors, and human sensors can produce uncertain and incomplete data [Berti-Equille et al., 2011, 2015] which become conflicting and whose veracity is difficult to check;

- Limits of information extraction: Techniques for extracting facts, events, entities, and relations from unstructured or loosely structured texts may have relatively low precision and may be difficult to parameterize and train; procedures for systematic checking and measurement of extractors' quality can be lacking or inappropriate. Similarly to the blocking problem in entity resolution, conflicting assertions may be extracted and grouped together by mistake even though they do not actually refer to the same fact or the same real-world entity, inversely data referring to the same real-world entity may be not grouped in the appropriate block, generating conflicts when the value is actually misfielded;

- Limits of data integration: Data integration of heterogeneous data sources may lead to inconsistencies at the instance-level due to inappropriate heuristics or techniques for schema and data mapping, data transformation, and record linkage;

- Ambiguity and uncertainty: Data semantics can be different and inconsistent from one information source to another, sometimes leading to misinterpretation, sometimes because of national or cultural differences in the usage of certain codes or symbols. This problem can affect both information extraction and data integration stages.

- Data staleness: When obsolete data are not eliminated, conflicts with more recent data can occur. This is also the case when data are replicated on various sites and the secondary copies are not updated in conformance with the primary copy. Without timestamp and data lineage metadata, it remains difficult to find out which version of the data value is the correct one, and even more difficult to capture precisely the up-to-datedness of a large collection of online sources.

- Data falsification and source collusion: False or distorted information can be intentionally propagated by one source or a coalition of sources. Information can be manipulated, biased, or presented selectively (e.g., omitting the context or occulting some data) to influence the audience and encourage a particular conclusion. Sources can potentially collude to give more weight or credibility to some information actually true or not. There may exist "copycat" sources that copy information from other sources, eventually introducing some changes [Dong et al., 2010a,b], or even "adversary" sources, who may deliberately give wrong information, either due to malice or error and misinterpretation. A common strategy to evaluate the reliability of the sources is to take advantage of data redundancy, and rely on majority voting heuristic, which simply assigns a true label to data that are claimed by the majority of the sources. But this strategy is known to be error-prone, because it counts all the sources equally and does not consider source dependence or collusion.

One can bet that the great diversity of these problems related to truth discovery will continue to interest various research communities for a long time.

1.3   CLASSIFICATION OF TRUTH DISCOVERY APPROACHES

Current approaches for evaluating the veracity of data will be thoroughly presented in this book. We classify them across a 2-dimensional space illustrated in Figure 1.2 where the scope and the type of content are considered.

- **Content-based approaches** mostly represented by fact-checking and data fusion methods aim at iteratively computing and updating a trustworthiness score of a source as a function of the belief in its claims, and then the belief score of each claimed data as a function of the trustworthiness of the sources asserting it. In these approaches, source quality is initialized and updated based on the content belief. In this context, several probabilistic models have been proposed to incorporate various aspects beyond source trustworthiness and data belief. These methods and related algorithms operate on structured data and they will be described

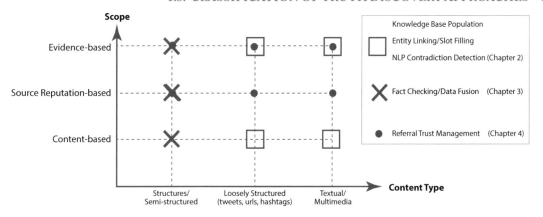

Figure 1.2: Main approaches for truth discovery. Content-based, recommendation-based, and evidence-based approaches operate on three types of content, from structured and semi-structured data to loosely structured information and textual and multimedia content.

in Chapter 3. For textual content, information extraction methods developed for knowledge base slot filling, entity linking, and contradiction detection will be presented in Chapter 2.

- **Recommendation-based approaches** mainly rely on the notion of community-based reputation of the sources as a public estimation of standing for merit, achievement, or reliability of the sources. Alternatively, reputation is the opinion (or a social evaluation) of a community toward a data provider. These approaches may also rely on popularity of the sources and trust management mechanisms that promote rewards for honesty and good past behavior and penalties for deceit. These methods and related algorithms for referral trust management will be described in Chapter 4.

- **Evidence-based approaches** generally extend content-based approaches and rely on external evidence, context, and *a priori* knowledge either about the sources or the content from a community/network of actors. In this context, data provenance information may be used in truth discovery computation, as well as external information about the context, the sources, the data, or the user network. The evolving nature of this evidence requires taking into consideration the dynamics of information in the network and revising truth discovery computation accordingly. Some advanced methods for data and knowledge fusion and fact-checking will be presented at the end of Chapter 3.

In Figure 1.2, the scope axis defines that the core of the approach mainly relies on: (1) the evaluation of the source characteristics, expertise, or qualities, (2) the content provided by the source, or (3) (external) evidences or ratings. The type of content is declined in three categories based on its structuration: from structured and semi-structured data, loosely structured entities, to free text or multimedia content.

The book is organized as follows. The second chapter **Information Extraction** provides a comprehensive survey on the state-of-the-art of methods that automatically extract entities and their relationships from textual corpora. We will present their principles, techniques, and applications to demonstrate how these methods are used for truth finding from texts. The third chapter **Truth Discovery Computation** provides a comprehensive survey of existing algorithms for automatic fact-checking for structured data, mainly used in data and knowledge fusion. The fourth chapter **Trust Computation** describes the main features of trust management and defines the concepts of trust, trustworthiness, source reputation, and related metrics. We will present different techniques from the literature for modeling and inferring trust. The fifth chapter **Misinformation Dynamics** will provide a broad outline of past and recent theoretical research, mainly from Statistical Physics, around diffusion dynamics in networked systems because it is critical to capture the temporal dimension of data veracity. The last chapter **Transdisciplinary Challenges of Truth Discovery** concludes this book by summarizing current contributions to the field. In this chapter, we touch upon some cutting-edge open problems for discovering truth in settings where information from multiple sources is rapidly evolving, eventually distorted, and propagated. We discuss how close we are to meeting these challenges and identify many open problems for future research. The next sections will provide an overview of the content of the main parts of the book. The breadth of this book is admittedly beyond a single discipline: the variety and extent of the "veracity challenges" call for a cross-disciplinary effort which motivates our incursions into several disciplines to review somewhat arbitrarily the related work we found relevant.

1.4   INFORMATION EXTRACTION

To automate the process of ascertaining the veracity of unstructured information, content processing is a first necessary step. Traditional information extraction pipelines require several analysis stages, ranging from text preprocessing (e.g., to split the input text into sentences, tokenize the sentences, lemmatize the tokens, tag their part-of-speech, normalize, etc.) to entity linking and relation extraction. Entities, attributes, and relations have to be detected, classified, linked across multiple documents possibly in different languages. Each stage of textual content analysis (preprocessing, entity linking, classification, slot filling) may produce systematic and random errors that need to be considered and mitigated later on in the truth discovery computation. Although a number of methods and toolkits have been developed for information extraction and knowledge base population, it is still difficult to determine which techniques are best suited, as each task is highly data dependent. Supervised techniques use carefully hand-crafted lists of terms and regular expressions, rather than corpus-trained unsupervised approaches. Each system typically performs very differently for different data sets and domains. Chapter 2 will present the state-of-the-art methods for information extraction, and knowledge base populations with entity linking and slot filling tasks that are particularly relevant for truth discovery from texts.

1.5 FACT-CHECKING AND TRUST COMPUTATION

As online user-generated content grows exponentially, the reliance on Web data and information from social media and social networks is growing in many domains for a variety of private as well as corporate usages. In this context, the challenge of truth discovery from multi-source data is intellectually and technically interesting enough to have attracted a lot of prior studies, both from database and artificial intelligence communities, sometimes investigated under the names of fact-checking [Goasdoué et al., 2013], information trustworthiness [Thirunarayan et al., 2014], information credibility [Pasternack and Roth, 2013], information corroboration [Galland et al., 2010], truth finding [Li et al., 2012], or data and knowledge fusion [Dong et al., 2014b].

In Chapter 3, we present one major line of research work which consists of iteratively computing and updating the source quality as a function of the belief in its claims, and then the belief score of each claim as a function of the trustworthiness of the sources asserting it. Detailed description of current models, assumptions, and algorithms for truth discovery computation incorporating prior knowledge about the claimed assertions or about the sources will be presented with a particular emphasis on probabilistic models. These have been proposed to incorporate various aspects beyond source trustworthiness and claim belief, such as: the dependence between sources [Dong et al., 2010b], the correlation of claims [Pochampally et al., 2014], the temporal dimension in discovering evolving truth [Dong et al., 2009b], the difficulty of ascertaining the veracity of certain claims, or the management of complex data structures or collections of entities within a claim [Zhao et al., 2012]. This chapter describes thoroughly the main approaches for evaluating the veracity of data on a discrete timeline, and also introduces recent contributions relaxing modeling assumptions from previous work, e.g., related to truth existence [Zhi et al., 2015] and approximate truth discovery [Li et al., 2014, Wang et al., 2015a]. New developments related to truth evolution [Li et al., 2015b], incremental truth discovery [Jia et al., 2013], truth discovery from data streams [Zhao et al., 2014], and truth discovery in crowdsourcing applications [Gao et al., 2015b, Ma et al., 2015] will also be presented in this chapter.

In Chapter 4, we survey the work on trust management and trust propagation. Trust in social recommender systems can be defined as one's belief toward others in providing accurate ratings relative to the preferences or view of the active user. We present the main concepts, metrics, and models for binary and multi-valued, direct and indirect trust computation with their theoretical underpinnings. Various reputation mechanisms from the literature of collaborative and social recommender systems will be reviewed and illustrated. Finally, this chapter will review current trust propagation mechanisms and offer the smooth transition to the next chapter where misinformation propagation is considered.

1.6 MISINFORMATION DYNAMICS IN NETWORKED SYSTEMS

Most of the information generated online is spread within a networked framework: except for blogs, our Web 2.0 experience happens in well-structured environments: Twitter, Facebook, Instagram, Whatsapp, etc. The historically large geographical and time scales that described news dissemination have literally vanished with the recent *socialization* of our digital experience—from passive information consumers to active generators of content. This revolution has had of course many consequences. On the scientific side, it poses serious challenges to understand diffusion processes. The speed capabilities and the size of the network on which information travels are unprecedented, and therefore new efforts have to be made for the understanding of new phenomena. On the social side, again speed and size give plenty of room for misinformation to travel and dwell within such systems: such is the downside of otherwise exciting advancements. In particular, a social network user is now exposed to sometimes noisy, sometimes biased, sometimes plain false information. The consideration of the previous problems has been approached from different stances. A good deal of work has been published with a strong theoretical accent, capitalizing on previous knowledge from other areas (such as epidemic spreading). Others have instead a marked empirical orientation, proposing heuristic approaches to deal with real-world problems—scalable solutions to deliver interpretation at reasonable cost.

Chapter 5 provides a broad outline of both extremes, and also whatever lies in between (to the authors' best knowledge). After a brief introduction to complex networks, the chapter reviews on the theoretical side past and recent research, mainly from Statistical Physics literature, around diffusion dynamics in complex networked systems. This includes epidemic spreading (mainly included for historical coherence) and rumor spreading. Analytical insights will be provided when these are possible, such as the determination of a critical threshold [Pastor-Satorras and Vespignani, 2001], i.e., the point at which a disease (or a rumor) goes global. We believe that it is critical to understand and capture the dynamics of (mis)information for evaluating its veracity. These contributions are complementary to several approaches for capturing data provenance but have not yet been considered in data integration and truth discovery research.

Associated with such a general framework (spreading dynamics), we encounter more specific problems: *source identification* and the problem of *influence*. These issues are already in contact with empirical problems, i.e., they have been tested against real-world data. In the complex networks discipline, source identification has been put forward with epidemic settings in mind to answer the following questions: Given a current snapshot of the diffusion of a certain disease, is it possible to trace it back to "patient zero"? How reliable could that inference be? On the other hand, the quest to understand influence has a practical side—how far will a disease or a piece of information travel, given the influence of those who spread it?—along with a sociological aspect—what defines an influential entity? Why does a certain entity become influential? This is a far-from-settled issue: good "reach predictors" for a certain propagating dynamics might behave badly in other setups [Borge-Holthoefer and Moreno, 2012, Kitsak et al., 2010]. The literature around this topic is divided in different approaches (from highly theoretical to purely applied), and they will be reviewed in a succinct and comprehensive manner with concrete examples to illustrate their differences. Finally, we provide an overview of practical problems, the main one being meme-mutation dynamics: how information mutation (i.e., changes in the phrasing form and/or changes in the truth value) affects the level of noise in a system, and how this can be dealt with. We specifically go through the work of [Leskovec et al., 2009], which pioneered a line of research trying to cope with fuzzy representations of a piece of information.

Overall, Chapter 5 is *not* about a finished corpus of work; it rather attempts to expose different approaches to data dissemination (the *forward problem*) and data provenance (the *inverse problem*) in a (social) networked environment—attempts which sometimes, unfortunately, do not connect (mainly because they are mutually unaware of). Thus, the chapter is implicitly delineating future opportunities, which hopefully will foster future developments.

CHAPTER 2

Information Extraction

2.1 INTRODUCTION

Traditional information extraction (IE) pipelines extract information from unstructured documents using Natural Language Processing (NLP) resources such as on lexicons and grammars. From 1987 to 1997, the Message Understanding Conferences (MUC) [Grishman and Sundheim, 1996] have shaped early work in IE. MUC and post-MUC IE systems can be characterized with three dimensions [Chang et al., 2006]:

- the structure of the content the systems can be applied to: from free texts, hand-written or CGI-generated HML, XML, tweets to database records;

- the techniques used for text processing: e.g., tag-level or word-level encoding for input string tokenization, scan pass, extraction rules and patterns, type and number of features involved, and learning algorithms; and

- the automation degree which defines the user involvement in collecting the training corpus, labeling the training examples, generalizing the extraction rules, and extracting the relevant data.

With the increasing volume of available textual information, much effort has been devoted to automate the tasks for collecting information from large-scale heterogeneous corpora where conflicting information may be provided by multiple sources [Barbosa et al., 2015]. Along with Web technology advances, IE has recently evolved into three domains that are of particular interest for truth discovery.

- Open IE that processes online semi- and unstructured documents applying machine learning and pattern mining techniques to exploit the syntactical patterns and layout structures of the documents. Open IE has achieved notable successful results on massive, open-domain English corpora from the Web in particular for identifying relations [Etzioni et al., 2008].

- IE from social media and microblog content where unusual structures and representations of discourse can switch between one-to-one to multi-party conversations and broadcast messages. These approaches are more adequate for microtexts (e.g., tweets) than traditional IE and can handle a wider language variation, unorthodox capitalization, frequent use of emoticons, abbreviations, and hashtags despite loose grammatical structure [Bontcheva et al., 2013].

- Knowledge Base Population (KBP) with Entity Discovery Linking (EDL) and Slot Filling (SF) tasks initiated by the U.S. National Institute of Standards and Technology (NIST) in the Text Analysis Conferences (TACs). The main goal of KBP is to gather information about an entity (e.g., a person or a company) that is scattered among a large collection of heterogeneous documents, and then use the extracted information to populate an existing knowledge base (KB). An Entity Discovery and Linking (EDL) system clusters the queries and decides whether the cluster corresponds to an entry in the knowledge base. A Slot Filling (SF) system extracts from a large collection of documents the values of specified attributes ("slot types") of a particular entity (e.g., date of birth of Steve Jobs, job position of Marissa Mayer, number of employees of IBM) and determines whether each value is true or false based on evidence collected from sentences in the texts that detail the context.

From a truth discovery perspective, we are particularly interested in the last body of research work on Entity Linking and Slot Filling and Chapter 2 will survey relevant contributions in this field. This chapter does not pretend to offer an exhaustive view of the very active domain of IE. It is meant instead to provide a concise summary of methods, models, and algorithms that are useful for end-to-end truth discovery from textual resources.

Since the performances of EDL and SF systems highly depend on the information extraction pipeline, we will first briefly describe it in the next section. Typically, information extraction includes a sequence of tasks for text processing, segmentation, normalization, and semantics analysis, including the recognition of named entities and the detection of mentions, coreferences, and relations between entities.

2.2   INFORMATION EXTRACTION PIPELINE

Natural language processing toolkits have increasingly gained popularity in the recent years. Many libraries, APIs, and large-scale multi-function toolkits along with various tutorials, textbooks and coding examples are currently available.[1] The complete IE pipeline illustrated in Figure 2.1 includes (1) text segmentation and grammatical tagging, (2) normalization, and (3) semantics analysis. The pipeline usually consists of the following main resources for linguistic processing: language identifier, tokenizer, sentence splitter, part-of-speech tagger, normalizer, gazetteer lists, named entity tagger (based on built-in regular expressions over annotations language), mention detector, and orthographic and coreference resolvers.

Each stage of the IE pipeline or component can be implemented using existing libraries or toolkits such as the most widely used ones presented in Table 2.1.

In the next sections, we will briefly review each main step of information extraction mainly because it is important to understand that errors in the IE process may utlimately have dramatic consequences on truth discovery and they need to be mitigated.

---

[1]See LingPipe competition list, accessed on Sept. 2015: http://alias-i.com/lingpipe/web/competition.html

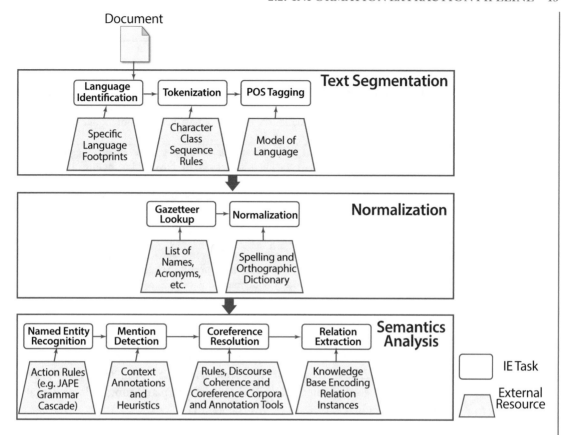

Figure 2.1: Generic information extraction pipeline.

2.2.1   TOKENIZATION AND SENTENCE SEGMENTATION

Text segmentation is an essential task of any NLP system where the goal is to divide a text into linguistically meaningful units—from characters (or graphemes) to words consisting of one or more characters, and sentences consisting of one or more words. The words and sentences identified at this stage are the fundamental units passed to further processing stages such as morphological analyzers, part-of-speech (POS) taggers, parsers, and information retrieval systems. Tokenization (also known as word segmentation) and sentence segmentation are two interdependent tasks which consist in locating the boundaries of the words and the sentences, respectively.

Tokenization consists of canonicalizing tokens so that matches occur despite differences in the character sequences of the word. Once hyphens are removed, they are grouped into equivalence classes (e.g., *anti-democratic* and *antidemocratic* are mapped to *antidemocratic*). Stemming and lemmatization reduce inflectional forms of the words and derive the canonical form of the

Table 2.1: Frameworks and toolkits for information extraction

GATE (General Architecture for Text Engineering) [Cunningham et al., 2002, 2013]	An open-source Java-based NLP framework including a number of rule-based NLP components and wrappers for developing NLP pipelines
UIMA (Apache Unstructured Information Management Architecture) [Ferrucci and Lally, 2004]	A Java-based framework with Eclipse plug-ins to define the component architecture and software framework implementation for the analysis of unstructured content like text, video, and audio data
NLTK (Natural Language Toolkit)[Loper and Bird, 2002]	A Python library for developing NLP applications with in-built classifiers such as Naive Bayes, Maximum Entropy, and binary tree classifiers
OpenNLP[2]	An open source providing components for sentence detection, tokenization, part-of-speech tagging, phrase chunking, syntactic parsing, named entity recognition, and coreference resolution
Stanford CoreNLP[3]	A Java suite that integrates part-of-speech tagging, named entity recognition, coreference resolution, sentiment analysis, and other bootstrapped pattern learning tools

words (e.g., *cars, car's, car* are mapped to *car*). Stemming removes the end of the word based on predefined rules. For example, Porter's algorithm rule defines the following mappings to transform the end of the word (e.g., *IES → Y: minorities → minority, SSES → SS, addresses → address*). Lemmatization is stemming based on dictionary; it uses vocabulary and morphological analysis of words to remove the inflectional ending to return the lemma.

Example 2.1   Consider the following input text: "*President Obama on Sunday pressed the nation of his father's birth to root out corruption, treat women and minorities as equal citizens, and take responsibility for its own future. (July 26) AP.*" Table 2.2 presents the output of three stemming algorithms applied to this input text.

2.2.2   NORMALIZATION

Normalization is commonly proposed as a solution for overcoming or reducing linguistic noise and name variance. Multiple representations of the same entity may cause ambiguities and conflicting values, and the normalization task transforms information to a standard format defined by the user. The task is generally composed of two steps: first, the identification of orthographic errors in the input text, and second, the correction of these errors and the transformation of abbreviations. As a first step, it usually combines spelling-correction dictionaries and heuristics to suggest correct spellings based on text edit distance and phonetic distance that can be used to find candidate

---

[3]OpenNLP, https://opennlp.apache.org/
[3]Stanford CoreNLP, https://github.com/stanfordnlp/CoreNLP

Table 2.2: Example of three stemming algorithms

Algorithm	Text
Porter [Porter, 1997]	Presid Obama on Sundai press the nation of hi father s birth to root out corrupt treat women and minor as equal citizen and take respons for it own futur Juli 26 AP
Lancaster [Paice, 1990]	presid obam on sunday press the nat of his fath ' s bir to root out corrupt , tre wom and min as eq cit , and tak respons for it own fut . (july 26) ap
Snowball [Agichtein and Gravano, 2000]	presid obama on sunday press the nation of his father ' s birth to root out corrupt , treat women and minor as equal citizen , and take respons for it own futur . (juli 26) ap

matches for words identified as misspelled. The second step is typically achieved through the use of conversion rules that produce a preselected standard format. For instance, to normalize time and date strings to standardized month, day, and/or year values, an IE system may enforce the TIMEX2 format as yyyy–?mm–?dd: e.g., "New Year's Day 2001" would be normalized as "2001–?01–?01." If a full date cannot be inferred using document text and metadata, partial date normalizations can be allowed using "X" for the missing information. For example, "March 4th" would be normalized as "XXXX–?03–?04"; "2001" would be normalized as "2001–?XX–?XX"; "the early 1900s" would be normalized as "19XX–?XX–?XX."

Normalization is usually included in the consistency component of the IE pipeline that makes use of various external resources encoding world knowledge such as: (1) a gazetteer with data extracted from various dictionaries including pronouns, common words, location names (e.g., Geonames[4]), vehicle and company names, nouns extracted from WordNet (e.g., hyponyms of PERSON), and mappings scrapped from Wikipedia (e.g., mappings from countries to nationalities); (2) a list of nicknames and acronyms used in approximate name matching (e.g., from AllAcronyms[5]); (3) the Wikipedia cross-lingual dictionary [Spitkovsky and Chang, 2012]; and (4) cross-document references where the documents including both the acronyms or synonyms and the full names are retrieved from the corpus and used for name expansion and unification.

Normalization also includes removing accents and diacritics (i.e., any mark, point, sign or glyph) and case-folding either based on heuristics, statistical approaches (e.g., tRuEcasIng [Lita et al., 2003]), or machine learning methods to decide whether some words should be in lower or upper case [Bikel et al., 1999].

2.2.3 PART-OF-SPEECH TAGGING

POS tagges mark each words in a text with labels corresponding to the part-of-speech of the word in its grammatical context. For example, Stanford log-linear POS tagger [Toutanova et al., 2003]

---

[4]Geonames, http://www.geonames.org/
[5]AllAcronyms, http://www.allacronyms.com/tag/city

is based on statistical and rule-based approaches trained using large corpora manually labeled with typical tags as illustrated in Table 2.3.

Table 2.3: Example 2.1 tagged by Treebank POS Tagger of NLTK [Loper and Bird, 2002]

Tagged text	President/NNP Obama/NNP on/IN Sunday/NNP pressed/VBN the/DT nation/NN of/IN his/PRP$ father/NN's/-NONE- birth/JJ to/TO root/NN out/IN corruption/NN ,/, treat/VB women/NNS and/CC minorities/NNS as/RB equal/JJ citizens/NNS ,/, and/CC take/VB responsibility/NN for/IN its/PRP$ own/JJ future/JJ ./.. (/-NONE- July/NNP 26/CD)/-NONE- AP/-NONE-
with tag list:	NN (Noun, singular), NNS (Noun, plural), NNP (Proper noun, singular), NNPS (Proper noun, plural), DT (Determiner), VB (Verb, base form), VBD (Verb, past tense), VBG (Verb, gerund or present participle, IN (preposition or subordinating conjunction), JJ (adjective), CC (conjunction, e.g., "and," "or"), PRP (Personal pronoun), MD (modal auxiliary, e.g., "can," "will"), etc.

2.2.4   NAMED ENTITY RECOGNITION

Named entity recognition (NER) in texts, such as news, is a very well-studied problem [Marrero et al., 2013, Nadeau and Sekine, 2007, Roberts et al., 2008, Wang et al., 2012a]. It consists in identifying and classifying some types of information elements, called Named Entities (NE) [Ratinov and Roth, 2009]. Concrete types of semantics such as PERSON, ORGANIZATION, LOCALIZATION, or temporal (date/time) and numerical (money, percentage, quantity) expressions are given and the goal of NER is to locate the elements in the text that fit the semantics. The evaluation of NER tools has been carried out in various conferences such as MUC,[6] CoNLL[7] [Tjong Kim Sang and De Meulder, 2003], and ACE[8] [Strassel et al., 2008] and special tracks of other venues, e.g., INEX Entity Ranking track (XER) [Demartini et al., 2010], TREC Entity Track (ET) [Balog et al., 2010], and TAC Knowledge Base Population task (KBP) [Ji and Grishman, 2011].

A number of applications have been deployed for entity extraction from News. For example, Europe Media Monitor's News Explorer[9] gathers news, clusters related news stories, and extracts names, locations, general person-person relations, and event types. OpenCalais from Thomson Reuters[10] extracts a range of entity, relation, and event types from general and business news. Most of these approaches use hand-crafted lists of terms and regular expressions, rather than corpus-trained approaches. For instance, the Calais family of products currently recognizes 39

---

[6]Message Understanding Conferences
[7]Computational Natural Language Learning
[8]Automatic Content Extraction
[9]Europe Media Monitor's News Explorer, http://emm.newsexplorer.eu
[10]Open Calais, http://www.opencalais.com

different types of NE, among which we can find TV shows and sports leagues. Thing Finder, a commercial tool by Inxight, recognizes 45 predefined types of NER, among which there are some more unusual ones such as holidays and financial indexes. These tools mostly rely on existing NE hierarchies such as the one proposed by Sekine [2008], including more than 200 categories of NEs.[11]

Among the supervised learning algorithms for NER, a large body of work has been done using Hidden Markov Model (HMM), decision trees, Maximum Entropy Models (ME), Support Vector Machines (SVM), and Conditional Random Fields (CRF). Typically, supervised methods either learn disambiguation rules based on discriminative features or try to learn the parameter of assumed distribution that maximizes the likelihood of the training data.

2.2.5 MENTION DETECTION AND COREFERENCE RESOLUTION

Mention detection is defined as a language-dependent step of marking potentially coreferences in a text. It is followed by coreference resolution which is the process of linking detected mentions in groups referring to the same entity. Two types of models have been proposed for coreference resolution:

- The mention-pair models that combine two steps: (1) classification to decide whether two mentions are coreferent (or not) in a document and (2) clustering based on the previous pairwise decision to build a partition of the mention set into equivalence classes (coreference clusters) corresponding to different entities [Ng and Cardie, 2002, Soon et al., 2001]. Relational probability models were developed to capture the dependency between each of these classifications [McCallum and Wellner, 2004, Singla and Domingos, 2004]; and

- The entity-based models [Luo et al., 2004, Wick et al., 2009, Yang et al., 2004, 2008] that are trained to determine whether an active mention belongs to a preceding, possibly partially formed, coreference cluster. Hence, they can employ cluster-level features, (i.e., features that are defined over any subset of mentions in a preceding cluster), which makes them more expressive than mention-pair models.

Training instances are created from texts annotated with coreference information. For each pair of mentions and their closest preceding antecedents, instances are marked as positive and negative references. Based on the classification proposed by Ng [2004], we can distinguish existing coreference resolution systems based on the following characteristics:

- Corpus-based or knowledge-based: the coreference resolution procedure is either based on heuristics for hand-crafting models of discourse or based on resolution features that are learned from labeled training data;

- Semi-automated or fully automated mention detection and resolution process; and

---

[11]"The Definition of Sekine's Extended Named Entities," accessed on Sept. 2015, http://nlp.cs.nyu.edu/ene/version 7_1_0Beng.html

- Basic or advance set of features used in the coreference resolution process: from morphosyntactic and syntactic features to semantic features and domain-specific knowledge.

More specifically, after tokenization, POS tagging, normalization, and NER, each token (or word) w_i under consideration is associated with a number of linguistic features including: lexical features (e.g., tokens in a window of seven characters $\{w_{i-3}, ..., w_{i+3}\}$); capitalization features; grammatical POS tags; morphological features (e.g., w_i's prefixes and suffixes of length one, two, three, and four); gazetteers' features; semantic features (e.g., the named entity (NE) tag of a word obtained using for instance the Stanford CRF-based NE recognizer [Finkel et al., 2005]); and features for coreference model outputs' scoring. In practice, many features can be modeled after the systems of Bikel et al. [1999] or Florian et al. [2004]. Based on this set of features, the mention-pair and entity-mention coreference classifiers are trained using various algorithms such as SVM learning algorithm [Rahman and Ng, 2009], closest-first [Soon et al., 2001], best-first [Ng and Cardie, 2002], correlation clustering [Bansal et al., 2004], graph partitioning [McCallum and Wellner, 2004], Bell-tree-based clustering [Luo et al., 2004], or mention and cluster ranking [Rahman and Ng, 2009].

The example from Vittorio Castelli [2010] illustrated the complete IE pipeline where each sentence is segmented, each token is labeled with its semantic role (e.g., spouseOf, agentOf, parentOf, memberOf), named entities are detected and classified into PERSON, ORGANIZATION, TIME, EVENT_MEETING; the mention pairs are detected, e.g., "Wu Shu-Chen, wife, her, She" tokens are grouped into the same cluster #1 and the time mention is normalized as "20090527."

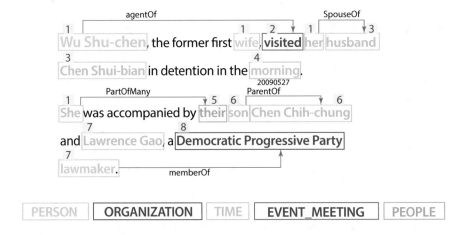

Figure 2.2: Mention detection and coreference resolution from Vittorio Castelli [2010].

2.3   KNOWLEDGE GRAPH POPULATION

KBP (Knowledge Base Population) is a process of discovering facts about entities from a large corpus to augment an incomplete knowledge base (KB) as input [Ji and Grishman, 2011]. There are two major tasks in KBP we will detail in the next sections: Entity Discovery and Linking (EDL) and Slot Filling (SF). Compared to traditional information extraction and query answering (QA) tasks, KBP focus is on resolving cross-document entity detection as well as redundant and conflicting answers from large corpora which is particularly relevant for truth discovery.

2.3.1   ENTITY DISCOVERY AND LINKING

Given a collection of documents, an EDL system is required to automatically extract (identify and classify) entity mentions (referred as queries), link them to existing entries in the knowledge base (KB), and cluster NIL mentions (with no corresponding KB entries). Recent EDL systems have to extract queries automatically. In this chapter, we focus on entity linking for the English language, rather than cross-lingual entity linking [Cassidy et al., 2012].

Typically, the task of entity linking is preceded by a named entity recognition step as described in Section 2.2.4. When performed without a knowledge base, entity linking reduces to traditional entity mention coreference as described in Section 2.2.5. In this line, one important research direction of the KBP program is "cold-start" with the goal to develop an automatic system to construct a KB from scratch. For more detail, we suggest the recent survey on entity linking systems by Shen et al. [2015].

Entity mentions detected in one or multiple documents are clustered into several different clusters each of which represents one specific entity.

In the database research community, this problem is related to the record linkage problem— also referred to as duplicate detection or entity resolution—which has been largely investigated for matching structured records that refer to the same real-world entity [Elmagarmid et al., 2007]. Compared to Entity Linking in KBP, the focus of DB research was rather on efficiency, scalability, and speed-up techniques for string similarity computation [Jiang et al., 2014] and duplicate record detection [Christen, 2012] whereas most earlier work on entity linking was formulated as a ranking problem [Ji et al., 2014] using either non-collective or collective approaches.

Non-collective approaches resolve one mention at a time using supervised learning models on local features, prior popularity, and context similarity [Mihalcea and Csomai, 2007, Milne and Witten, 2008].

Collective approaches disambiguate a set of candidate mentions simultaneously by leveraging the global consistency between entities through graph-based methods [Cassidy et al., 2012, Cucerzan, 2007, 2011, Huang et al., 2014, Liu et al., 2013, Shen et al., 2013].

A typical mono-lingual EDL system architecture has been summarized by Ji and Grishman [2011]. As illustrated in Figure 2.3, it includes six steps: (1) entity mention extraction to identify and classify entity mentions from the source documents; (2) query expansion to expand the query into a broader set of words using, for instance, Wikipedia structure mining or coreference resolution in the background document; (3) candidate generation to identify all possible entries in the knowledge base that are linked to the query; (4) candidate ranking using non-collective or collective approaches based on graph, rules, similarity or information retrieval; the linking decision can be used as feedback to refine the entity mention extraction results from step (1); and finally (4) NIL detection and clustering to detect and group into clusters the NILs with low confidence at matching the top KB entries.

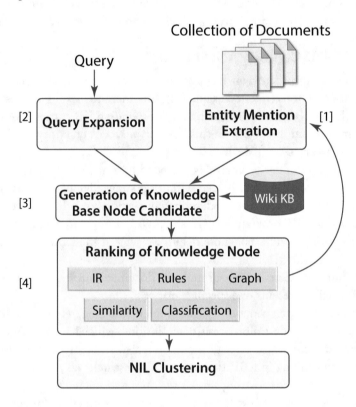

Figure 2.3: General entity discovery and linking system architecture adapted from Ji and Grishman [2011].

A large body of research has been done in parallel in the Wikification community [Bunescu and Pasca, 2006] which aims at extracting prominent *n*-grams as concept mentions, and link each concept mention to the knowledge base. However, in contrast to Wikification, EDL only focuses on three types of entities: Person (PER), Organization (ORG), and Geo-political Entity (GPE, a location with a government) and requires NIL clustering [Mihalcea and Csomai, 2007, Ratinov and Roth, 2012].

2.3.2 RELATION EXTRACTION AND INFERENCE

Relation extraction (RE) is the process of discovering useful relationships between entities mentioned in text [Agichtein and Gravano, 2000, Zelenko et al., 2003]. Traditional IE systems have focused on identifying instances of known relationships from small, domain-specific text corpora, e.g., news articles or job postings. But the user is required to explicitly specify each relation of interest, extraction patterns or positive and negative instances of the relation. This considerable manual labor makes traditional IE approaches neither scalable nor portable across a broad range of domains. To overcome these issues, various supervised, semi-supervised and unsupervised methods have been proposed (see [Konstantinova, 2014] for an overview) to perform mostly binary relation extraction from textual data. In RE in general and supervised RE in particular, a lot of research was done for IS-A relations and extraction of taxonomies using several available resources such as Wikipedia, [12] DBpedia, [13] Freebase,[14] YAGO,[15] and query logs. Particular techniques focus on higher order relations [Cheng and Roth, 2013].

Traditional IE systems based on manually developed extraction rules have been superseded by information extractors learned through training on supervised corpora [Lodhi et al., 2002]. There are different ways that extractors can be learned in order to solve the problem of supervised relation extraction. However, reliably extracting relations between entities in natural-language documents is still a difficult, unsolved problem. In the next sections we will review the main techniques for relation extraction such as kernel-based methods [Bunescu and Mooney, 2005a,b], logistic regression [Kambhatla, 2004], and Conditional Random Fields (CRF) [Culotta et al., 2006].

Kernel-based Methods

Various syntactic and semantic features can be extracted from a sentence to detect the representation of a relation. Semantic features like the dependency path between the two entities in the sentence have been used by Kambhatla [2004] maximum entropy model. Support Vector Machines (SVMs) have been used for feature selection among standard syntactic features in GuoDong et al. [2005]. Kernel-based methods have been widely used for relation extraction. The principle of string kernels initially proposed by [Lodhi et al., 2002] for text classification has been successfully applied to the problem of relation extraction in various approaches [Bunescu and Mooney, 2005b, Culotta and Sorensen, 2004, Zelenko et al., 2003]. The goal is to extract a subsequence of words or POS tags that represent a relation over two tokens and use all such anchored subsequences as features.

However, explicitly creating for each sentence a vector with a position for each such feature is infeasible, due to the high dimensionality of the feature space. Fortunately, dual learning algorithms can be exploited to process examples only via computing their dot product (or inner

---

[12]Wikipedia, `http://www.wikipedia.org`
[13]DBpedia, `http://dbpedia.org`
[14]Freebase, `http://www.freebase.com`
[15]YAGO, `http://yago-knowledge.org`

product in the Euclidean space) as the Support Vector Machines (SVMs). The dot product between two vectors is calculated as the number of common anchored subsequences between the two sentences.

A string kernel is a function that computes the inner product between two strings which are mapped to a given feature space. A q-gram spectrum kernel considers the feature space of q-grams (substrings of size q). For string S, let $\Phi_q(S) = (|Occurrence(S, p)|)_{p \in \Sigma^q}$ be the occurrence frequencies of all q-grams in S. The kernel function is computed by summing up the product of occurrence frequencies in strings S_1 and S_2 for all q-grams which occur in both S_1 and S_2 such as:

$$K_q(S_1, S_2) = \langle \Phi_q(S_1), \Phi_q(S_2) \rangle = \sum_{p \in \Sigma^q} |Occurrence(S_1, p).Occurrence(S_2, p)|.$$

This can be done in $O(q(|S_1| + |S_2|))$ time.

Tree kernels compute the structural similarity between sentences which have proven useful in predicting certain relation types. In the case of tree kernels, the subsequences are replaced by parse trees and similarity is computed between sentences. Tree kernels have been used for specific relations like person-affiliation and organization-location by Culotta and Sorensen [2004]. Bunescu and Mooney [2005a] refine the tree kernel approach by determining the dependency path between two entities that carries sufficient information to determine the relation between them. Bunescu and Mooney [2005b] use a bag-of-features kernel based on the idea that context around entities can be used to determine if a given relation exists between them.

Semi- and Unsupervised Methods for Relation Extraction

Because of the important shortcoming of supervised methods requiring labeled data to train classifiers, several systems have been proposed to address generic relation extraction as a semi-supervised or unsupervised problem.

Banko et al. [2007] proposed TextRunner which does not require the relation and its format to be specified as input. It consists of a pipeline of a learner, an extractor, and an assessor. The learner generates its own labeled training data and produces a trained classifier that can be used by the extractor. The learner uses dependency parsers and syntactic parsers as part of this process. The extractor then parses webpages and applies the classifier to each sentence containing entity pairs to detect and identify relations. Finally, the assessor assigns probabilistic confidence scores to extracted relations derived and thresholds weak relations.

Surdeanu et al. [2012] proposed MIMLRE system (Multi-instance Multi-label Relation Extraction) which employs distant supervision [Mintz et al., 2009] to train a model for extracting relations between two entities. Using existing structured data sources such as Freebase, DBPedia, the system identifies entity pairs that are involved in different relations of interest. It crawls and extracts any sentence containing the entity pairs identified in the previous step and labels it as a relationship between the two entities. Using these labeled candidate sentences, Surdeanu et al.

[2012] train a multi-label classifier to assign more than one relation for a given entity pair, which differs from most of the previous methods extracting only one type of relation.

Other unsupervised algorithms such as clustering [González and Turmo, 2009, Yan et al., 2009] have been used to perform relation extraction grouping entity pairs that belong to the same relation without using any seed data.

2.3.3   SLOT FILLING

Very similar to but considered to be less challenging than relation extraction, Slot Filling task consists of extracting values from identified the entity types restricted to PERSON and ORGANIZATION. Twenty-five relation types for PERSON entities and sixteen relation types for ORGANIZATION entities presented in Table 2.4 have been defined in the KBP slot filling task of Text Analysis Conference. No other relation types and corresponding entities are expected to be extracted in this task.

Table 2.4: KBP2014 slot names for the two generic entity types

Person	Organization
per:alternate_names	org:alternate_names
per:date_of_birth	org:political_religious_affiliation
per:age	org:top_members_employees
per:country_of_birth	org:number_of_employees_members
per:stateorprovince_of_birth	org:members
per:city_of_birth	org:member_of
per:origin	org:subsidiaries
per:date_of_death	org:parents
per:country_of_death	org:founded_by
per:stateorprovince_of_death	org:date_founded
per:city_of_death	org:date_dissolved
per:cause_of_death	org:country_of_headquarters
per:countries_of_residence	org:stateorprovince_of_headquarters
per:statesorprovinces_of_residence	org:city_of_headquarters
per:cities_of_residence	org:shareholders
per:schools_attended	org:website
per:title	
per:employee_or_member_of	
per:religion	
per:spouse	
per:children	
per:parents	
per:siblings	
per:other_family	
per:charges	

Stanford's slot filling system [Angeli et al., 2013, 2014] based on the DeepDive framework [Niu et al., 2012] includes three steps for KBP English Slot Filling task: (1) feature extraction, (2) constraint engineering, and (3) statistical inference and learning. Candidate sentences are extracted by distant supervision [Mintz et al., 2009] and their respective entity and relation mentions are derived. A Gibbs sampler is used to obtain relation probabilities over the derived factor graph. Freebase is used as training data source for distant supervision.

The slot filling system from University of Massachusetts UMass IESL [Roth et al., 2014] is also based on distant supervision to identify candidate sentences. It performs relation prediction using universal schema matrix factorization [Riedel et al., 2013] which extracts entity pairs, relations, and context between entities from candidate sentences and leverages the co-occurrence information.

Knowledge Vault system [Dong et al., 2014a] from Google aggregates information from different sources across the Web to build a knowledge base. They employ sixteen different relation extractors for a variety of heterogeneous information sources, e.g., text documents, HTML tables, HTML trees. The system then combines the output of four extraction methods by building a classifier [Reyzin and Schapire, 2006]. For each proposed fact, the classifier considers both the confidence value of each extractor and the number of documents found by the extractor.

2.3.4   SLOT FILLER VALIDATION

Since SF systems have various quality performances and can provide conflicting answers as illustrated in Table 2.5, a task for KBP Slot Filler Validation (SFV) has been proposed with the goal to evaluate and combine the output from multiple slot filling systems and use language processing to validate the results from different SF systems. The objective is to maximize the F1-score. In this context, several ensemble systems have been developed to combine results of various slot filling systems. However, this line of work is very interesting and tightly connected to the research on data fusion as we will describe in the next chapter.

In the 2013 JHUAPL system, Wang et al. [2013] uses the confidence values returned by individual SF systems with each extracted filler (i.e., value). They use constrained optimization to aggregate the individual confidence values and produce a single aggregated confidence score. This score is used to determine if the filler must be included in the final result.

In the UI CCG system developed as a trust-based SFV system, Sammons et al. [2014] aggregates results of multiple systems using majority voting. The system learns threshold values on the number of SF systems that extract a particular filler to decide whether it must be included in the result.

Sigletos et al. [2005] use stacking to combine the output of IE systems. This addresses the situation where most systems could be wrong in which case majority voting would fail. They exploit the disagreement between different IE systems by stacking them and report improved performance. Many KBP SFV systems cast validation as a single-document problem and apply a variety of techniques, such as rule-based consistency checks [Angeli et al., 2013] and techniques

Table 2.5: Example of conflicting answers from five slot filling systems for `per:country_of_birth` slot of Barak Obama from the same heterogeneous corpora

System	Slot Filler	Source	Evidence
S_1	Africa	`espectivas.wordpress.com/2008/11/07`	Barack Hussein Obama was born in Africa, and therefore he does not meet the US basic constitutional requirements to become President of The United States of America.
S_2	Africa	`westernjournalism.com`	Barack Hussein Obama was born in Africa
S_3	Hawaii	`mediamatters.org/research/2009/07/17`	President Obama was born in Hawaii, according to state officials, and copies of his certification of birth.
S_4	Mombasa	`mofopolitics.com/2009/07/27`	Obama's grandmother on phone states Obama was born in Mombasa, Kenya.
S_5	Africa	`canadafreepress.com/article/36024`	Obama was born in Africa, but his grandmother registered him with a COLB in Hawaii.

from the Recognizing Textual Entailment (RTE) task described in the next section. Some systems use rule-based consistency checks to perform filler validation. Angeli et al. [2014] employ such a scheme using a weighted constraint satisfaction problem (CSP) to maximize the sum of confidences of slot fillers subject to the manually specified constraints on slots.

Many SFV systems use provenance information to perform consistency checks and filter mechanisms. But it is possible to design features from provenance metadata that capture the agreement or disagreement between SF systems in a finer grained fashion as proposed by Viswanathan et al. [2015].

The RPI Blender KBP system [Yu et al., 2014, 2015] casts SFV in the truth discovery framework, using a graph propagation method that modeled the credibility of systems, sources, and response values. It employs multidimensional truth finding to filter candidate sentences that may express potential relations between target entities.

[Yu et al., 2014] proposed an unsupervised approach for slot filling validation, extending the co-HITS [Deng et al., 2009] method over heterogeneous networks composed, as illustrated in Figure 2.4, of three layers of sources, responses as pairs of claim and evidence, and slot filling systems.

Yu and colleagues proposed a credibility propagation technique as follows.

1. Initialize credibility scores c^0 for each source of the set of sources S to 1, similarly for each SF system in T with TextRank [Mihalcea and Tarau, 2004] and for each response in R using linguistic indicators.

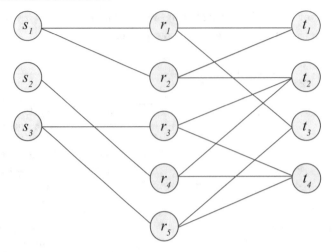

Figure 2.4: Heterogeneous network for credibility propagation in slot filling validation from Yu et al. [2014].

2. Construct heterogeneous networks across R, S, and T with transition probability:

$$p_{ij}^{rs} = \frac{w_{ij}^{rs}}{\sum_k w_{ik}^{rs}}$$

using the elements of the weight matrices W^{sr} and W^{rt}.

3. Compute:

$$\begin{cases} c(s_i)=(1-\lambda_{rs}C^0(s_i) + \lambda_{rs}\sum_{r_j \in R} p_{ij}^{rs}c(r_j) \\ c(t_k)=(1-\lambda_{rt}C^0(t_k) + \lambda_{rt}\sum_{r_j \in R} p_{jk}^{rt}c(r_j) \\ c(r_j)=(1-\lambda_{sr}C^0(r_j) + \lambda_{sr}\sum_{s_i \in S} p_{ij}^{sr}c(S_i) + \lambda_{tr}\sum_{t_k \in T} p_{kj}^{tr}c(t_k) \end{cases} \tag{2.1}$$

with λ_{rs}, λ_{rt}, λ_{sr} and $\lambda_{tr} \in [0,1]$, the control parameters used for defining the credibility propagation over initial score for every type of random walk link in the heterogeneous network. After normalization, each response's score $c(r_j)$ is influenced by both linked sources and systems. The propagation converges similarly to HITS algorithms [Peserico and Pretto, 2009]. As we will see in the next chapter, this solution takes into account the reliability of the extractor and slot filing systems and define the problem as an graph optimization problem that can be solved with an analytical approach such as in the Semi-Supervised Truth Finder (SSTF) method proposed in Yin and Tan [2011] presented in Section 3.3.3.

2.4   CONTRADICTION DETECTION

Since the PASCAL challenge in 2005, Recognizing Textual Entailment (RTE) has become a popular research topic in NLP research [Dagan et al., 2005]. This task requires a system to recognize, given two text fragments, whether the meaning of one text is entailed (i.e., can be inferred) from the other text. Textual entailment (TE) refers to a directional relation between two text segments or sentences. TE exists when the truth of one text segment follows from that of another. The goal of RTE is to classify the semantic relation between the Text and the Hypothesis into three categories: Entailment, Contradiction, or Unknown. A variety of techniques have been successfully employed in the RTE Challenge in order to recognize instances of textual entailment such as the example in Table 2.6 that requires in particular the understanding of spatial relations.

Table 2.6: Example from PASCAL RTE Challenge at TAC 2009 (RTE-5, development set, id224, text truncated)

T: Three major bombings in less than a week will be causing some anxiety among political leaders in Baghdad and Washington. Last Thursday 10 people were killed by a car bomb at a crowded cattle market in Babel province, south of Baghdad. On Sunday more than 30 died when a suicide bomber riding a motorbike blew himself up at a police academy in the capital. Tuesday's bombing in Abu Ghraib also killed and wounded a large number of people - including journalists and local officials.
H: Some journalists and local officials were killed in one of the three bombings in the Baghdad area.

Condoravdi et al. [2003] proposed the first entailment and contradiction metrics. Later on, de Marneffe et al. [2008] proposed a definition of contradiction for NLP tasks and developed available corpora, from which they constructed a typology of contradictions. Detecting genuine contradiction required deep inferential paths and background knowledge to overcome apparent contradictions, such as meronyms, synonyms, misfielded values, and polysemy as illustrated by the examples in Table 2.7.

Table 2.7: "Seeming" contradictions examples from Ritter et al. [2008]

Meronyms	BornIn(Mozart, Salzburg)
	BornIn(Mozart, Austria)
Synonyms	DiedFrom(Mozart, kidney failure)
	DiedFrom(Mozart, renal failure)
Misfielded value	BornIn(Mozart, Salzburg)
	BornIn(Mozart, 1756)
Polysemy	BornIn(John Smith, 1850)
	BornIn(John Smith, 1737)

In contrast to previous work which has mostly exploited "negation" and "antonyms," Au-Contraire Contradiction Detection (CD) system identifies "functional phrases" statistically [Ritter et al., 2008]. The system relies on TextRunner [Banko et al., 2007] that resolves numerous syntactic problems (e.g., anaphora, relative clauses) and semantic challenges (e.g., quantification, counterfactuals, temporal qualification) and identifies functional relations. Using background knowledge to filter out false positives in the contradiction detection task, the system automatically identifies functional relations, groups together extractions with the same argument and functional relation, but differing values.

The goal of the Statement Map project [Murakami et al., 2009] is to help Internet users evaluate the credibility of information sources by analyzing supporting evidence from a variety of viewpoints/opinions on their topics of interest. This work focuses on agreement and conflict recognition from subjective texts. They discussed how to efficiently collect valid examples from Web documents by splitting complex sentences into fundamental units of meaning called statements and annotating relations at the statement level. The conflict cases contained three finer-grained categories: contradiction, confinement, and conflicting opinion.

Vydiswaran et al. [2014] conducted a user study called BiasTrust to understand the factors that affect the perception of credibility of controversial claims, and how to overcome the human tendency to stick to one's own viewpoint. The authors varied different parameters to test which factors significantly help users to learn about a controversial topic.

2.5   CONCLUSION

In this chapter, we have surveyed the main approaches in information extraction from NLP processing to entity linking and slot filling, and also introduced critical tasks of information extraction that are relevant to truth discovery from unstructured text.

A number of applications, libraries, and toolkits have been deployed for information extraction. All differ along multiple dimensions and can perform very differently for different corpora and application domains. However, it is difficult to determine which techniques are best suited. There are many aspects that affect the design and performances of the entity linking and slot filling systems, starting from each task of the IE pipeline and depending on the characteristics of the documents.

Each stage of textual content analysis (from text preprocessing, to entity discovery and linking, relation extraction, and contradiction detection) may produce systematic and random errors that need to be considered and mitigated later on in truth discovery computation. The recent approaches on Slot Filling Validating consider the uncertainty from information extraction affecting the truth discovery and data fusion results and these recent advances coupled with ensembling methods for SFV are promising directions to address this issue.

CHAPTER 3

Truth Discovery Computation

3.1 INTRODUCTION

As online user-generated content grows exponentially, the reliance on Web data and information from social media and social networks is growing in many domains for a variety of private as well as corporate usages. But data can be incorrect, misleading, and eventually falsified. As the number of conflicting data usually increases with the number of information sources providing them, it is becoming more and more challenging to estimate the veracity of data.

The quality of data varies from one source to another and the reliability of each source is *a priori* unknown, variable, and heterogeneous (e.g., from one topic to another). The basic principle of truth discovery is to iteratively infer sources' reliability from the data it provides and estimate the veracity of data from the reliability of the sources claiming them. In line with this principle, a grand challenge in truth discovery is to design methods that can capture a wide range of (sometimes adversarial) scenarios where, for instance, most of data sources are not reliable or collude time-to-time to claim particular false information, given that the ground truth is largely unknown or out-of-reach.

Motivated by the great diversity and complexity of related problems but also by its direct applications in various contexts of information retrieval, data fusion, and decision-making, truth discovery has legitimately received an ever-increasing attention of researchers from various research fields in data science and also from Web industries, national intelligence and security agencies, and journalists [Cohen et al., 2011b].

In Chapter 2, we reviewed the main techniques for extracting information to obtain structured data and also approaches for filling an existing knowledge base with extracted and formatted information. This is important because the current chapter follows up on structured data and review the main contributions from data fusion research. In this context, a wealth of research with a great variety of methods has been produced for truth discovery from structured data and Chapter 4 will offer a comprehensive overview of existing work, presenting the algorithms and salient features of the current methods so that the readers can easily compare them and evaluate how appropriate and actionable each method can be for a given real-world scenario or data set.

The line of research that will be presented in detail in this chapter mainly covers the approaches which aim at iteratively computing and updating the trustworthiness of each data source as a function of the belief in the data it claims, and then the belief score of each claimed data as a function of the trustworthiness of the sources asserting it. First, we will introduce the terminology and present the main modeling assumptions underlying the current approaches. Then we will review the main truth discovery models that have been proposed to incorporate various aspects beyond source trustworthiness and claim belief in the context of structured data provided by multiple, explicitly identified sources.

3.2 TERMINOLOGY

Different terms for similar or identical concepts are commonly used in the literature on truth discovery. To keep terminology consistent throughout this chapter, we recap the main definitions in Table 3.1.

Table 3.1: Truth discovery terminology

Term	Definition
Fact	*A fact is a true claim.*
Allegation	*An allegation is a false claim.*
Claim	*A claim is a value provided by an identified source.*
Value	*A value refers to the value of a property of a real-world entity.*
Object	*An object refers to a real-world entity. An object can be described by multiple properties, attributes, or features.*
Data item	*A data item is a valued property for a given object instance.*
Source	*A source is a provider of data items.*
Mutual exclusive set	*A mutually exclusive set is a set of values claimed for a given object property by multiple sources.*
Source trustworthiness	*The trustworthiness (or accuracy or reliability) of a source is a score that quantifies how reliable the source is, given the confidence of its claims.*
Value confidence	*The confidence of a value is a score that quantifies the veracity of the value, given the trustworthiness of the sources claiming it.*
Truth label	*A truth label is a Boolean value determining whether the value of a claim for a given object property is true or false.*
Ground truth	*Ground truth (sometimes called golden standard) is the set of facts (i.e., values of object properties known to be true in the real world). This set is usually manually verified/labeled and used for quality performance evaluation of the truth discovery methods.*

Example 3.1

To illustrate this terminology, consider the example presented as a bipartite graph in Figure 3.1 including the name of the current presidents of four countries claimed by four information sources from S_1 to S_4.

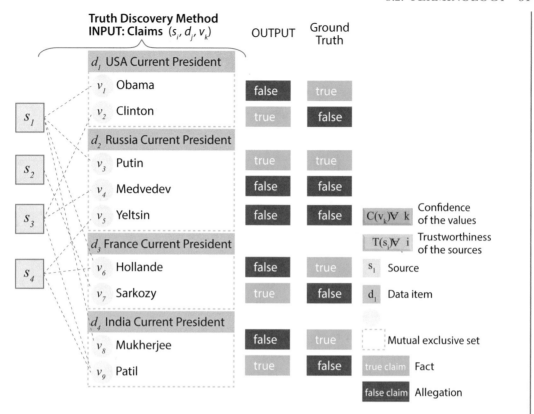

Figure 3.1: Illustration of the terminology via an example: Four sources provide the names of current presidents of USA, Russia, France, and India. The values are grouped into a mutual exclusive set for each data item. The input claim of a truth discovery method is a triplet of the identified source, the data item, and the claimed value. The output of the method is a Boolean label associated with each claim, the confidence of the claimed value and the source trustworthiness score for each source. The ground truth data set determines the facts (true claims) from the allegations and it is used for quality performance evaluation of the truth discovery method.

We consider the truth discovery algorithms that take, as input data, a set of structured claims in the form of triplets (sourceID,dataItemID,claimedValue), e.g., (S1,Russia.CurrentPresident,Putin) and infer, as main output result, a Boolean label for each claim. In addition, the truth discovery algorithms may also return T_s, the trustworthiness of each source, and C_v, the confidence of each value. Each data item is a uniquely identified pair of object-attribute. Values referring to the same data item (corresponding to a property of a real-world entity) are grouped into so-called *mutual exclusive set* where usually only one value for each data item is assumed to be true. Typically, the method output is composed of the labels for each claimed value with its corresponding confidence score and the trustworthiness score of each source. When the ground truth is available, the method output can be evaluated with the traditional quality performance metrics (i.e., accuracy, precision, recall, specificity, F1-measure) essentially based on counting the number of true (or false) positive (or negative) results.

Table 3.2: Illustrative example: name of current presidents claimed by four sources

		S_1	S_2	S_3	S_4	Ground Truth	Conflicts
d_1	USA	Obama	–	Clinton	–	Obama	2
d_2	Russia	Putin	–	Medvedev	Yeltsin	Putin	3
d_3	France	Hollande	Sarkozy	–	Hollande	Hollande	2
d_4	India	Mukherjee	–	Patil	Patil	Mukherjee	2
Source Coverage		1	.25	.75	.75		

Claims can also be represented in a tabular form such as in Table 3.2. In the example, nine distinct values for the four data items are claimed by the sources. The correct answer known as the *Ground Truth* is given in the sixth column of Table 3.2. Source coverage (last line of the table) represents the ratio of the number of values provided by the source over the total number of objects (e.g., the number of countries); in the example, source coverage is 1 for S_1, .25 for S_2, and .75 for S_3 and S_4. Only source S_1 provides a correct value for each data item, noted from d_1 to d_4, in conformance with the ground truth. The number of distinct values per object is reported in the last column Conflict of the table—e.g., d_1, d_3, and d_4 data items have two distinct values. We will see later on that source coverage and conflict distribution play an important role in truth discovery computation.

In this example, we could apply majority voting to find the true values but this may be misleading in case of a tie (e.g., d_1) or when some sources copy claims from each other (e.g., S_4 may copy d_3's value from S_1 and d_4's value from S_3).

Moreover, we can easily understand that the veracity of some claims may be more difficult to ascertain depending on our background knowledge. For example, if only one source claims a value, it would be more difficult to estimate whether this value is true or not without any other external evidence. Finding the truth may actually require some background knowledge, for instance, if you consider Spain and United Kingdom that do not have a president but a prime minister. In that case, no true value actually exists for data items such as Spain.CurrentPresident or UK.CurrentPresident. We will see in Section 3.4 that these cases respectively refer to the notion of claim hardness (i.e., the difficulty of estimating the veracity of certain claims) and truth cardinality when sometimes none of the values claimed by the sources is true [Zhi et al., 2015].

3.2.1 NOTATIONS AND BASIC PRINCIPLE

We use the notations given in Table 3.3. In particular, S_v denotes the set of sources providing value v, and $S_{\bar{v}}$ represents the set of sources providing a distinct value from v for the same data item. Similarly, we use the index $._v$, $._s$, or $._d$ to refer respectively to value v, source s, or data item d. For instance, D_s denotes the set of data items covered by source s, V_s is the set of values provided by source s, and V_d denotes the set of values provided for data item d. V_{D_s} is the set of all values provided by source s for the set of all data items this source covers.

Table 3.3: Notations

S	Set of all sources
S_v	Set of sources providing value v
$S_{\bar{v}}$	Set of sources providing a distinct value from v
S_d	Set of sources providing a value for data item d
D	Set of data items as (object, attribute) pairs
D_s	Set of data items covered by source s
D_v	Set of data items corresponding to value v
V	Set of all values for all data items
V_d	Set of values provided for data item d
V_{D_s}	Set of values for the data items covered by source s
l_v	Boolean truth label of value v
V_s	Set of values provided by source s
T_s	Trustworthiness of source s
C_v	Confidence of value v

As illustrated in Figure 3.2, the core of a fact-finder is an iterative, transitive voting algorithm: First, the trustworthiness of each source is initialized. For each object and each data item, the method calculates the confidence of each claim from the reliability of its sources. Then it updates the trustworthiness of each source from the confidence of the claims it makes. The procedure is repeated until the stopping condition is satisfied. Usually, the stopping criterion is defined either as a maximum number of iterations or a threshold under which the variability of the results (i.e., value confidence or source trustworthiness scores) are considered to be stable from one iteration to the next. In this case, the algorithm terminates. Some methods start with initializing the confidence scores of the values instead of the source trustworthiness, then compute source trustworthiness and update value confidence scores in a similar way.

3.2.2 CHARACTERIZATION OF TRUTH DISCOVERY METHODS

As a part of the comprehensive review of the truth discovery literature, we propose a characterization of the truth discovery methods based on four dimensions, accommodating a wide spectrum

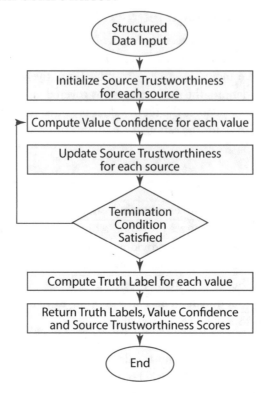

Figure 3.2: Basic iterative algorithm for truth discovery.

of existing methods of truth discovery from structured data. The main dimensions are related to the characteristics of: the method, the data input, the prior knowledge, and the output result.

Method Features
To select the most appropriate method, it is important to consider the inherent characteristics of the method.

(a) **Initialization and parameter setting**: some methods require complex parameterization and careful initialization; in these cases, a ground truth data set is often necessary to tune the parameter setting (e.g., LTM [Zhao et al., 2012], Depen [Dong et al., 2009a]).

(b) **Repeatability**: some methods use randomized sampling or random initialization (e.g., LTM [Zhao et al., 2012], FAITCROWD [Ma et al., 2015]); averaging multiple execution runs of these methods is required to get good estimates of the final results but these multiple executions need to be considered when comparing time complexity and total execution time of the methods.

(c) **Convergence and stopping criterion**: Methods may require specific termination conditions or functions to ensure convergence (e.g., 3-ESTIMATES [Galland et al., 2010]); some methods may have no convergence guarantee.

(d) **Complexity and scalability**: The baseline complexity is $O(|S|.|V|)$ which corresponds to time complexity of majority voting algorithm that is highly scalable to very large data sets but does not consider finer-grained analysis of the claimed values or the sources' characteristics; ultimately a trade-off between efficiency/scalability, modeling assumptions, and accuracy needs to be defined by the user to capture real-world scenarios [Wang et al., 2015a].

(e) **Trainable/non-trainable or unsupervised/semi-supervised**: Some methods require a training data set to learn and estimate hidden variables whereas other methods are totally unsupervised. As an example, the majority voting is a non-trainable and unsupervised baseline method with repeatable results, converging at the stopping criteria that can be predefined as a fixed number of iterations or with a threshold condition on the cosine similarity of the source trustworthiness scores between two iterations.

Data Input

Truth discovery methods also differ in the data set characteristics they can handle, such as the following.

(a) **Data type**: some methods take as input categorical, nominal (string/text), or numerical data values, whereas other methods require careful data preprocessing and transformation to convert the data into Boolean values, e.g., the claim (`c1,S1,Russia.CurrentPresident,Putin`) has to be transformed as (`c1,S1,Russia.CurrentPresident:Putin,Yes`) for MLE [Wang et al., 2012b].

(b) **Cardinality of claims**: some methods can handle indifferently mono- and multi-valued claims (i.e., list of values) but other methods only accept mono-valued claims which requires data input transformation; e.g., a claim such as (`c2,S1,USA.Last3Presidents,(Obama,Clinton,Bush)`) has to be transformed into three mono-valued claims such as (`c21,S1,USA.Last3Presidents,Obama`), (`c22,S1,USA.Last3Presidents,Clinton`), and (`c23,S1,USA.Last3Presidents,Bush`) (e.g., LTM [Zhao et al., 2012]).

(c) **Value similarity**: some methods take into account the case of similar strings or textual values claimed for a given data item and consider them as mutually supportive claims in the process of truth computation (e.g., TRUTHFINDER [Yin et al., 2008] and AccuSim [Dong et al., 2009a]).

(d) **Correlations between values, attributes, and objects**: some methods incorporate external knowledge that encodes relationships between the values, for example based on meronomy or taxonomy relations, e.g., *"Obama is born in Hawaii"* and *"Obama is born in the USA"* are mutually supportive claims. Correlations between attributes and objects may also be used to quantify how supportive or disconfirming claims can be for a given data item or object and some methods reinforce or penalize the value confidence scores accordingly (e.g., [Pochampally et al., 2014].

Prior Knowledge

Important modeling assumptions underly every truth discovery method in particular related to the following.

(a) **Source quality characteristics** such as dynamics, distribution, and homogeneity: (1) The source quality can be considered constant or evolving depending on the method's assumptions; (2) Source quality distribution can be initialized either uniformly across all the sources or specifically for each source (e.g., LCA [Pasternack and Roth, 2013]). So depending on our prior knowledge of the quality of sources, we may select methods that allow source-specific quality initialization or if we have rather a global view of the sources' quality (i.e., when all the sources are likely to equally provide true information), we may opt for methods that initialize sources' trustworthiness uniformly; (3) Most of the methods consider that source quality is homogeneous across all the data items. In other words, homogeneous source quality means that each source is likely to provide true information with the same probability for all the objects and attributes it claims; most of existing methods have this assumption and have to be adapted to capture heterogeneity of the source quality across data items.

(b) **Dependence between sources**: some methods can estimate the copying relationship probability between each pair of sources and integrate this estimate in the computation of the accuracy of the sources (e.g., [Dong et al., 2009a]). The main goal is to detect and eventually penalize dependent sources which may collude to promote certain values.

(c) **Hardness of certain claims**: the veracity of some claims is sometimes more difficult to estimate and some methods can capture this particular prior knowledge (e.g., 3-ESTIMATES [Galland et al., 2010]).

Output

The output of any truth discovery method is commonly the truth label and confidence score of each valued claim and the trustworthiness score of each source but existing methods can differ in three aspects.

(a) **Single vs. multiple true value**: few methods can handle multiple true values for a given data item (e.g., LTM; Zhao et al. [2012] or Wang et al. [2015b]).

(b) **None or at least one true claim**: few methods can detect that none of the claimed values is true (e.g., Zhi et al. [2015]).

(c) **Explanation and evidence enrichment** may be provided by some methods (e.g., Dong and Srivastava [2013], Waguih et al. [2015]).

As we will see in the rest of the chapter, there is no "one-size-fits-all" solution for truth discovery computation from structured data. The choice of one truth discovery method actually depends on the aforementioned dimensions to better characterize the truth discovery scenario, data set, and user's prior knowledge and requirements. Table 3.4 summarizes along these dimensions the methods from the literature that we will further describe in the next sections.

Time Complexity
Table 3.5 presents the time complexity of the main methods we reviewed in this chapter.

3.2.3 MODELING ASSUMPTIONS

All truth discovery methods rely on several modeling assumptions related to the sources, the input claims, and the output result. The common principle of current methods is that trustworthiness of a source is a function of the truth values of its claims. Claims from at least one but generally from multiple sources are considered by the methods. As a consequence, a value claimed by only one source is assumed to be true by default (although the user can change this default parameter). Most importantly, a substantial overlap of the sources' coverage across multiple data items is needed for all existing methods to get meaningful results. In other words, if there is no (or very few) data items in common with values claimed by multiple sources, the results of all current methods will not be reliable as empirically demonstrated with synthetic data by [Waguih and Berti-Equille, 2014]. Several other important assumptions come into play.

- **Assumptions about the sources**. Three main modeling assumptions concern the sources: (1) Sources are assumed to be self-consistent and non-redundant. This means that a source does not claim conflicting values for the same data item. Additionally, the source should not provide duplicate claims. As a consequence, the quality of data preprocessing and data preparation is critical, and not removing all approximate and eventually conflicting duplicate claims from the same source will introduce bias or even invalidate the results; (2) Another important assumption is that the probability a source asserts a claim is independent of the truth of the claim. For example, some sources may choose to stay silent except when giving trivial or "easy" truths and this will lead to a very high trustworthiness score for these sources, although they do not deserve it; (3) Current methods rely on trusting the majority and they are well-adapted for situations where not only the sources are assumed to be predominantly honest but also when the number of sources providing true claims is assumed to be significantly larger that the number of sources providing false claims, which we refer to as the "optimistic scenario" assumption for truth discovery.

Table 3.4: Method characterization

Dimension	Subdimension	Methods						
		TRUTH-FINDER	3-ESTI-MATES	MLE	SimpleLCA	LTM	DEPEN	SSTF
Method	Complex parameter setting	No	No	No	No	Yes	Yes	Yes
	Repeatability	Yes	Yes	Yes	Yes	No[a]	Yes	Yes
	Convergence	Yes	Yes	No[b]	No[c]	No[d]	Yes	Yes
	Scalability	Yes	Yes	No	No	No	No[e]	Yes
	Trainable	No	No	No	No	Yes	No	Yes
Data input	Data Type (String, Categorical, Numerical, Boolean)	S,C,N	S,C,N	B	S,C,N	S,C,N	S,C,N	S,C,N
	Mono/multi	Mono/Multi	Mono/Multi	Mono	Mono/Multi	Mono	Mono/Multi	Mono/Multi
	Similarity	Yes	No	No	No	No	Yes	Yes
	Correlations	No	No	No	No	No	No[f]	No
	Source Quality	Constant, Uniform	Constant, Uniform	Constant, Source-specific	Constant, Source- and data item specific	Incremental, source-specific	Constant, uniform and Source-specific	Constant, uniform
Prior knowledge	Source Dependence	No	No	No	No	No	Yes	No
	Claim Hardness	No	Yes	No	Yes	No	No	No
	Single/Multi-Truth	Single	Single	Single	Single	Multi-truth	Single	Single
Output	At least One/No truth	At least One	At least One	At least One	At least One	At least One/No Truth	At least One	At least One
	Explanation, Enrichment	No	No	No	No	No	No	No

[a] Requires averaging over multiple executions
[b] Requires user-defined K iterations
[c] Idem
[d] Idem
[e] extended in Li et al. [2015a]
[f] extended in Pochampally et al. [2014]

Table 3.5: Time complexity per iteration of truth discovery algorithms

	Value Confidence Computation	Source Trustworthiness Computation	Time Complexity per Iteration
Voting	$|S_v|.|V|$	–	$|S_v|.|V|$
TruthFinder	$|S_v|.|V|$	$|S|.|V_s|$	$|S|.|V| + |V_d|^2$
Cosine	$|S|.|V| + |V|$	$|S|.|V| + |S|$	$|S|.|V|$
2-Estimates	$|S|.|V| + |V|$	$|S|.|V| + |S|$	$|S|.|V|$
3-Estimates	$|S|.|V| + |V|$	$|S|.|V| + |S|$	$|S|.|V|$
LTM	$|S.|V|$	–	$|S|.|V|$
MLE	$|S|.|V|$	$|S|.|V_s|$	$|S|.|V|$
Depen	$|S_v|^2.|V|$	$|S|.|V| + |S|^2.|V_s|^2$	$|S|^2.|V_s|^2$
Accu	$|S_v|^2.|V|$	$|S|.|V| + |S|^2.|V_s|^2$	$|S|^2.|V_s|^2$
AccuSim	$|S_v|^2.|V|$	$|S|.|V| + |S|^2.|V_s|^2$	$|S|^2.|V_s|^2 + |V_d|^2$
SimpleLCA	$|S|.|V|$	$|S|.|V_s|$	$|S|.|V|$

- **Assumptions about the input claims.** (1) The extraction of structured claims (including entity and relation discovery, linking, and resolution) is assumed to have no error (except in Dong et al. [2014a]); (2) Only claims with a direct source attribution are considered. This requires that a source of a claim should be explicitly identified with a direct correspondence between each source and its claim. Consequently, current methods do not consider cases such that "S_1 *claims that S_2 claims A*"; (3) Moreover, claims are assumed to be positive: e.g., "*S claims that A is false*" or "*S does not claim A is true*" are not considered and this can be a critical problem when the claim has been extracted from a text without the context and even without the negation. Few methods (e.g., LCA [Pasternack and Roth, 2013]) consider claim uncertainty and can handle cases such as "*S claims that A is true with 15% uncertainty.*"

- **Assumptions about the output result.** (1) Each claim is assumed to be either true or false. Although value confidence score is generally returned as output by every method, truth labeling is binary usually with no contextual information or additional evidence; (2) One important assumption about the claims is that the assertions made by the sources are organized per data item into disjoint mutual exclusion sets and only one of the claims in each set is generally assumed to be true. However some methods relax this assumption and can handle multi-truth scenarios (e.g., LTM [Zhao et al., 2012] or [Wang et al., 2015b]) where none of the values claimed by the sources is actually true [Zhi et al., 2015].

Relaxing these assumptions constitutes a very challenging research agenda on its own and this requires formally defining the semantics of truth discovery for realistic, operational, and actionable scenarios.

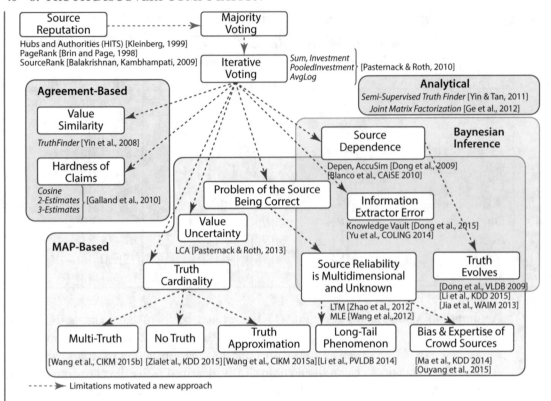

Figure 3.3: Evolution of truth discovery research: a roadmap of the methods from the literature.

3.3   TRUTH DISCOVERY METHODS

In this section, our goal is to provide a more detailed description of existing truth discovery methods that we classify into four categories based on the particular computational technique that underlies the truth computation.

1. **Agreement-based methods** mainly rely on the counting of the number of agreeing/disagreeing sources for each data item.

2. **Maximum A Posterior (MAP) estimate-based methods** rely on Expectation-Maximization or Gibbs sampling to compute the optimal latent variables (i.e., the truth label and source honesty or reliability) based on available observations.

3. **Analytical methods** use matrix diagonalization to solve truth discovery reformulated as a graph optimization problem.

4. **Bayesian inference-based methods** rely on Bayesian probabilistic modeling to compute source accuracy and value confidence.

MAP Estimate-based and Bayesian methods can be both represented as Plate diagrams, however the way they solve the truth discovery problem is totally different, which is why we did not choose to classify them undistinctively as probabilistic graphical models as other authors did [Gao et al., 2015].

This classification results from the observation of the evolution of the algorithms aiming to overcome some of the limitations of previous approaches and also to relax some of the modeling assumptions we mentioned earlier. This evolution is illustrated in Figure 3.3.

Source reputation models initially proposed by the research community on trust analysis focused on the evaluation of the popularity and authoritativeness of the sources but this was not sufficient and fine-grained enough for estimating the veracity of the content claimed by the sources. Authoritative sources may be wrong (e.g., on February 28, 2015, AFP [Agence France-Presse], a famous international news agency erroneously reported the death of the Bouygues conglomerate CEO) and on the other side of the spectrum, some non reputable sources (e.g., microblogs, discussion forums, or social medias) can be trusted because they provide true and relevant information about particular topics (for example, "blog for a cure"[1] provides a correct description of side-effects for some cancer medical treatments).

As a consequence, not only source reputation but also claims have been considered. Due to the shortcomings of majority voting as we will explain in the next section, a large body of work has been directed to improve iterative voting algorithms to incorporate the notion of similar and mutually supportive claims, along with the notion of hardness of claims and value uncertainty. Because source reliability is unknown and multidimensional, some approaches have been proposed to capture it along with the truth label and prior knowledge as latent variables with MAP estimation-based methods. In order to better capture source collusion and dependence, Bayesian inference methods have been proposed [Blanco et al., 2010, Dong et al., 2009a, 2010b] and further extended to solve other problems such as correlation between attributes [Pochampally et al., 2014], information extraction errors [Dong et al., 2014a], multi-truth-finding problem where multiple true values may hold for a single data item [Wang et al., 2015b] and evolving truth [Dong et al., 2009b].

3.3.1   AGREEMENT-BASED METHODS

The agreement-based methods can be divided into two major groups.

- The first group of methods refers to the approaches from Web link analysis and trust metrics (See Levien [2004] for a review of the trust metrics). They generally consist in computing the relative importance of a source in the Web graph based on the probability of landing on the source node by a random surfer. HUBS AND AUTHORITIES (HITS) [Kleinberg, 1999],

---

[1]http://www.blogforacure.com/

PageRank [Brin and Page, 1998], and SourceRank [Balakrishnan and Kambhampati, 2011] are well-known representative approaches.

- The second group of methods relies on the iterative voting algorithm which iteratively computes the source trustworthiness as a function of the confidence scores of the values it claims, and the confidence score of a value is a function of its source trustworthiness. Methods such as Sum (adapted from HITS), Average.Log, Investment, PooledInvestment proposed by Pasternack and Roth [2010], TruthFinder [Yin et al., 2008], and Cosine, 2-Estimates, 3-Estimates proposed by Galland et al. [2010] enter in this category.

Table 3.6 presents the functions used by the agreement-based methods to compute iteratively source trustworthiness and value confidence. As you can see the formulas are more and more complex to take into account source trustworthiness of previous iterations, using normalization (e.g., Avg.Log), and linear combination or exponential increase of the vote count of the value with respect to the sum of the invested trustworthiness (e.g., Investment).

Table 3.6: Agreement-based methods and their iterative score computation (with i, the number of iterations)

Method	Initialization	Source Trustworthiness T_s and Value Confidence C_v
Sum	$C_v^0 = .5$	$T_s^i = \sum_{v \in V_s} \omega(s, v) C_v^{i-1}$ and $C_v^i = \sum_{s \in S_v} \omega(s, v) T_s^i$ with $\omega(s, v)$ the uncertainty of source s in its claim v
Average.Log	$C_v^0 = .5$	$T_s^i = \frac{\log(\|V_s\|)}{\|V_s\|} \cdot \sum_{v \in V_s} C_v^{i-1}$ and C_v^i same as Sum
Investment	$C_v^0 = \frac{\|S_v\|}{\sum_{d \in V_d} \|S_d\|}$	$T_s^i = \sum_{v \in V_s} \left(\frac{C_v^{i-1} T_s^{i-1}}{\|V_s\| \sum_{r \in S_v} \frac{T_r^{i-1}}{\|V_r\|}} \right)$ and $C_v^i = \left(\sum_{s \in S_v} \frac{T_s^i}{\|V_s\|} \right)^{1.2}$
Pooled Investment	$C_v^0 = 1/\|V_d\|$	T_s same as Investment; $C_v^i = H_v^i \cdot \frac{(H_v^i)^{1.4}}{\sum_{r \in V_d} (H_r^i)^{1.4}}$ with $H_v^i = \sum_{s \in S_v} \frac{T_s^i}{\|V_s\|}$

TruthFinder	$T_s^0 = .8$	$T_s^i = Avg_{v \in V_s}\left(1 - e^{-\gamma C_v^i}\right)$ and $C_v^i = \sum_{s \in S_v} -\ln\left(1 - T_s^{k-1}\right)$
Cosine	$C_v^0 = 1$	$T_s^i = .8 * T_s^{i-1} + .2 \dfrac{\sum_{v \in V_s} C_v^{i-1} - \sum_{d \in D_s, v \in V_d \backslash V_s} C_v^{i-1}}{\sqrt{\sum_{d \in D_s} |V_d| \cdot \sum_{d \in D_s, v \in V_d} (C_v^{i-1})^2}}$ $C_v^i = \dfrac{\sum_{s \in S_v} (T_s^i)^3 - \sum_{s \in S_d \backslash S_v} (T_s^i)^3}{\sum_{s \in S_d} (T_s^i)^3}$
2-Estimates	$T_s^0 = 1$	$T_s^i = \dfrac{\sum_{v \in V_s} C_v^i + \sum_{d \in D_s, v \in V_d \backslash V_s} (1 - C_v^i)}{\sum_{d \in D_s} |V_d|}$ and $C_v^i = \dfrac{\sum_{s \in S_v} T_s^{i-1} + \sum_{s \in S_d \backslash S_v} (1 - T_s^{i-1})}{|S_d|}$
3-Estimates	$T_s^0 = 1, T_v^0 = .9$	$T_v^i = \dfrac{\sum_{s \in S_v} \frac{C_v^i}{1 - T_s^{i-1}} + \sum_{s \in S_d \backslash S_v} \frac{1 - C_v^i}{1 - T_s^{i-1}}}{|S_d|};$ $T_s^i = \dfrac{\sum_{v \in V_s} \frac{C_v^i}{1 - T_v^i} + \sum_{d \in D_s, v \in V_d \backslash V_s} \frac{1 - C_v^i}{1 - T_v^i}}{\sum_{d \in D_s} |V_d|}$ and $C_v^i = \dfrac{\sum_{s \in S_v} T_s^{i-1} T_v^{i-1} + \sum_{s \in S_d \backslash S_v} (1 - T_s^{i-1} T_v^{i-1})}{|S_d|}$

As illustrated in Figure 3.4, we use the simple Sum fact-finder on our previous example 3.1 with source trustworthiness and value confidence defined in Table 3.6. Initially, we believe in every claim equally and set C_v^0 to 1 for iteration $i = 0$. The first iteration compute the trustworthiness of each source based on the summation of the confidence scores of its claims. We assume every source is certain about the claim they make, i.e., $\omega(s, v) = 1$ for each s. In the example, $S2$ trustworthiness equals 2 since it provides two values with confidence score 1 each. Then confidence scores are updated based on the sum of their respective source trustworthiness scores. For instance, the new confidence score for "Obama" value is then 5, summing trustworthiness scores of $S4$, $S5$, and $S6$. The following two iterations updates each source trustworthiness and each claim confidence similarly. After three iterations, the maximal confidence score determines the true value for each data item: for the example, "Yeltsin," "Obama," and "Hollande" are selected to be the true values of the current presidents of Russia, United States, and France respectively.

Initialization: We believe in each claim equally: $\forall v, C^0(v)=1$

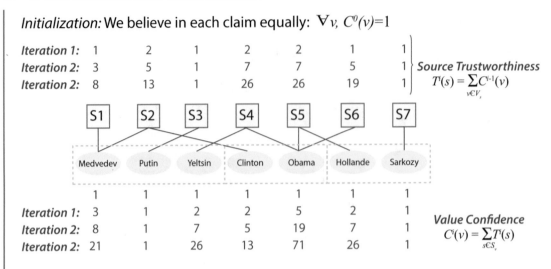

Figure 3.4: Illustrative example using Sum fact-finder.

Limit of Majority Voting Accuracy

All the agreement-based methods rely on the majority voting principle (also known as the plurality vote). In this scheme, for a given data item, the value that is supported by the highest number of sources (the most frequent vote) is considered to be true. Assume that c distinct values claimed by different sources are given as c-dimensional vectors $[a_{i,1}, \ldots, a_{i,c}]^T \in \{0, 1\}^c$ with $i = 1, \ldots, |S|$ where $a_{i,j} = 1$ if source s_i claims value v_j, and 0, otherwise, and $|S|$ the number of sources. The majority vote will return value v_k if

$$\sum_{i=1}^{|S|} a_{i,k} = \max_{j=1..c} \sum_{i=1}^{|S|} a_{i,j}.$$

Ties are resolved arbitrarily. It will indeed coincide with the simple majority (50% of the votes +1) in the case of two distinct values ($c = 2$). Assume now that the number of sources, $|S|$, is odd and the probability for each source to give the true claims is p for any object. The sources' claims are independent, that is for any set of sources $A \subseteq S, A = \{S_{i_1}, \ldots, S_{i_K}\}$,

$$P(S_{i_1} = v_{s_{i_1}}, \ldots, S_{i_K} = v_{s_{i_K}}) = P(S_{i_1} = v_{s_{i_1}}) \times \ldots \times P(S_{i_K} = v_{s_{i_K}}), \tag{3.1}$$

where $v_{s_{i_j}}$ is the value of source s_{i_j}.

According to the previous equation, the majority vote will give an accurate result if at least $\lfloor |S|/2 + 1 \rfloor$ independent sources give correct claims ($\lfloor x \rfloor$ denotes the "floor," which is the nearest integer smaller than x). Then the accuracy of majority vote is

$$P_{MV} = \sum_{m=\lfloor |S|/2+1 \rfloor}^{|S|} \binom{|S|}{m} p^m (1-p)^{|S|-m} \tag{3.2}$$

The following result is also known as the Condorcet Jury Theorem (1785). This theorem, originally written to provide theoretical basis of democracy, refers to a jury of voters who need to make a decision regarding a binary outcome (for example to convict a defendant or not). This theorem is very interesting for truth discovery in general and agreement-based methods in particular for the following reason: for p, the probability of the sources being correct and P_{MV}, the probability of the majority of sources being correct in Equation 3.2,

1. If $p > 0.5$, then $P_{MV} > 0.5$ and P_{MV} is monotonically increasing, $P_{MV} \to 1$ as $|S| \to \infty$.

2. If $p < 0.5$, then P_{MV} is decreasing and $P_{MV} \to 0$ as $|S| \to \infty$.

3. If $p = 0.5$, then $P_{MV} = 0.5$ for any $|S|$.

This result supports the intuition that we can expect improvement over the individual accuracy p only when p is higher than 0.5. This theorem shows two major limits of the accuracy of majority voting: the first is related to the requirement that the sources must be independent which is often difficult to determine and the second is related to the two possible outcomes depending on the probability of the sources being correct which is usually unknown and not necessarily uniformly distributed across all data sources. Nevertheless, if these two preconditions are met, then a correct decision can be obtained by simply selecting the value claimed by the largest number of sources.

However, in the example of the current presidents, we can see that other limitations related to the definition of the stopping criterion, the convergence which may not be guaranteed and other considerations related to value similarity have actually motivated a large body of work for improving the iterative voting baseline and overcoming its limitations.

TruthFinder

Among the agreement-based methods, TRUTHFINDER proposed by Yin et al. [2008] computes the confidence of a claim as the probability of being true and the truthworthiness of the source (website) as the expected confidence of its claims. The main idea behind TRUTHFINDER is that a claim is likely to be true if it is provided by trustworthy sources, and a source is trustworthy if most of its claims are true. As presented in Algorithm 3.3.1, the method was the first to incorporate the notion of similar supportive values to enhance the vote count of a value by the vote counts from its similar values. It uses a weighted function with a control parameter ρ and in the same time compensates, with the dampening factor γ, the effect of mutual supportive claims that are claimed by dependent sources.

Algorithm 3.3.1: T TRUTHFINDER$(S, D, V, \rho, \gamma, \delta)$

Initialization. $\forall s \in S : T_s \leftarrow 0.8$
repeat
$\left|\begin{array}{l} \textbf{for each } d \in D \\ \quad \textbf{do} \left\{\begin{array}{l} \textbf{for each } v \in V_d : \\ \quad \textbf{do} \left\{\begin{array}{l} \sigma_v \leftarrow - \sum\limits_{s \in S_v} \ln(1 - T_s) \\ \sigma_v^\star \leftarrow \sigma_v + \rho \sum\limits_{v' \in V_d} \sigma_{v'}.sim(v, v') \\ C_v \leftarrow \frac{1}{1+e^{-\gamma \sigma_v^\star}} \end{array}\right. \end{array}\right. \\ \textbf{for each } s \in S \\ \quad \textbf{do } T_s \leftarrow \frac{1}{|V_s|} \sum\limits_{v \in V_s} C_v \end{array}\right.$
until $Convergence(T_S, \delta)$
for each $d \in D$
$\quad$ **do** $trueValue(d) \leftarrow \underset{v \in V_d}{\operatorname{argmax}}(C_v)$

In TRUTHFINDER algorithm, initially, the truthworthiness of each source, T_S, is uniformly set to .8. TRUTHFINDER relies on the honesty of the sources and follows the heuristics that a source providing mostly true claims for many data items will likely provide true claims for other objects. The error rate of the source is $(1 - T_s)$. Instead of accumulating trustworthiness scores as in SUM-like methods, TRUTHFINDER computes the vote count as a product of trustworthiness $\prod_{s \in S_v}(1 - T_s)$ and use the natural logarithm product rule. Following this general idea, the confidence score of a value in TRUTHFINDER is $\sigma_v = -\sum_{s \in S_v} \ln(1 - T_S)$ and the source truthworthiness is the average, $T_s = \sum_{v \in V_S} C_v/|V_S|$. Logarithm is used to avoid underflow of the truthworthiness when the quantities are small. Additionally, TRUTHFINDER adjusts the confidence score of a claim so that it incorporates the influence (or support) that similar claims may have mutually on each other with $\sigma_v^\star = \sigma_v + \rho \sum_{v' \in V_d} \sigma_{v'}.sim(v, v')$.

For instance, for a multi-valued data item, a source providing the claim (AuthorA,AuthorB) for a particular book will support another source that provides the claim (AuthorA,AuthorB,AuthorC) for the same book (but not inversely). The weight of such support between the values is controlled by the parameter $\rho \in [0, 1]$.

The final confidence of a claim is then computed using a logistic function, $C_v = \frac{1}{1+e^{-\gamma.\sigma_v^\star}}$. The damping factor γ compensates the effect when sources with similar values are actually dependent. In that case, the confidence of supporting claims is overestimated and the dampening factor has to be tuned with no *a priori* knowledge of source dependence. Since TRUTHFINDER computes similarity between values, it can be dramatically affected by the number of distinct values to compare which explains relatively lower performance when the number of conflicts is high. Finally, as a stopping criterion, TRUTHFINDER uses the difference of source truthworthiness cosine similarity between two successive iterations to be less than or equal to a given threshold, δ. The value with the highest confidence is then selected as the true value among the other (false) values for a given data item.

Information Corroboration

In the category of agreement-based methods, COSINE, 2-ESTIMATES, and 3-ESTIMATES algorithms have been proposed by Galland et al. [2010].

For each data item d and value v, COSINE considers the value as a vector with dimension $|S|$ and position value 0 if source s_j does not claim the value v for d, -1 if s_j claims another value and 1 if s_j claims v. COSINE computes the truthworthiness of a source as the cosine similarity between the vector of its provided values and similarly it computes the vector of probabilistically selected values. As presented in Table 3.6, it iteratively computes source truthworthiness as a linear combination of the truthworthiness achieved in the previous iteration. For each claimed value, the value confidence is computed as a function of the current truthworthiness scores of the sources claiming this value minus the truthworthiness scores of disagreeing sources.

2-ESTIMATES computes source trustworthiness by averaging value counts. As in COSINE, 2-ESTIMATES takes into consideration disagreeing sources for every data item while computing the value confidence as a function of both agreeing and disagreeing sources claiming different values. This method requires a complex normalization for the vote counts and source trustworthiness to the range of [0,1]. As a stopping condition, the authors used a fix point computation for testing convergence.

3-ESTIMATES improves over 2-ESTIMATES by considering additionally trustworthiness of each value (noted T_v in Table 3.6) and representing the likelihood that a vote on this value would be correct. The measure is computed iteratively together with source trustworthiness and value vote count with similar normalization and convergence testing functions.

3.3.2   MAP ESTIMATION-BASED METHODS

A family of methods that rely on Maximum A Posterior (MAP) estimation have been proposed including MLE [Wang et al., 2012b], LCA [Pasternack and Roth, 2013], and LTM [Zhao et al., 2012]. LCA and MLE rely on Expectation Maximization as underlying technique to find the latent variables that maximize the expectation of a claim correctness given the source reliability. These approaches differ from the agreement-based methods mainly in the modeling of the source trustworthiness. In the agreement-based methods, source trustworthiness is explicitly defined by a measure (see Table 3.6) but since it is a complex, unknown concept, MAP estimation-based methods rather capture it as a latent variable to estimate. In the three models, LCA, MLE, and LTM a fixed number of iterations has to be specified with no guarantee that the convergence can be reached at the end of the execution; on the other hand, the convergence can be reached before the fixed number of iterations.

Maximum Likelihood Estimation

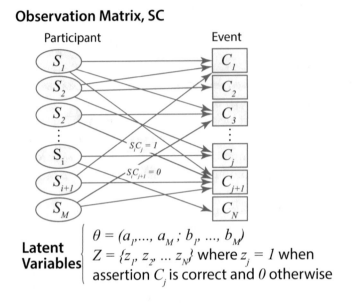

Observation Matrix, SC

Figure 3.5: Plate diagram of MLE from Wang et al. [2012b].

Maximum Likelihood Estimation (MLE) proposed by Wang et al. [2012b] is based on the Expectation Maximization (EM) algorithm to quantify the reliability of sources and the correctness of their observations. MLE has been applied to the context of social sensing where participants observe certain events (for instance, litter in a park). These observations are modeled as a matrix illustrated in Figure 3.5. The goal of MLE is to maximize the expected probability that a source provides a correct report of an existing event, given the participant reliability. MLE defines participant (or source) reliability with two parameters, namely:

- a_i is the probability that source i reports a value given that it is a true value; and

- b_i is the probability that source i reports a value given that it is a false value given d, the truth prior.

These parameters are defined as:

$$a_i = \frac{t_i \times s_i}{d}$$

and

$$b_i = \frac{(1 - t_i) \times s_i}{1 - d}$$

with s_i the speak rate of the participating source i defined as $s_i = P(S_i C_j)$ that represents the probability that source i does not remain silent when noticing an event and t_i is the reliability that participating source i correctly reports the event j as a joint probability such as $t_i = P(C_j^{true}|S_i C_j)$ for source i and event report correctness j.

MLE starts with initializing the sources' parameters: a_i and b_i. MLE uses Expectation step to compute the expected probability that the event reported by the source (i.e., observation SC) is correct (z) given each source reliability parameters (θ):

$$Q(\theta|\theta^{(t)}) = E_{Z|SC,\theta^{(t)}}\left[\log \sum_z P(SC, z|\theta)\right]$$

MLE iteratively computes the conditional probability of a value v to be true based on its source reliability parameters (a_i, b_i) and on the probabilities of the sources not providing v ($\forall j \in S_{\bar{v}}$). Then it iteratively computes the confidence of each value.

In the Maximization step, MLE updates the sources probabilities a_i and b_i and computes:

$$\theta^{(t+1)} = argmax_\theta\left(Q(\theta|\theta^{(t)})\right)$$

MLE only deals with Boolean positive observations. Negative observations are ignored. MLE considers in the same way a source claiming a negative value and a source having nothing to claim about the data item. Consequently, MLE requires the transformation of the input claims into Boolean mono-valued claims. For example, the claim (S1,USA.CurrentPresident,Obama) has to be transformed into the claim (S1,USA.CurrentPresident.Obama,Yes).

Latent Credibility Analysis

Latent Credibility Analysis (LCA) proposed by Pasternack and Roth [2013] is a model that also uses the Expectation Maximization algorithm to calculate the probability of a claim being true, by grouping claims related to the same data items into mutual exclusion sets where only one true claim exists. True claim is modeled as a multinomial latent variable. Similarly to MLE, LCA models use Expectation Maximization to find θ^*, the maximum a posteriori point estimate of the parameters such as: $\theta^* = \arg\max_\theta P(X|\theta)P(\theta)$ and then computes $P(Y_U|X, Y_L, \theta^*) = \frac{P(Y_U,X,Y_L|\theta^*)}{\sum_{Y_U} P(Y_U,X,Y_L|\theta^*)}$ with Y_U the unlabeled claims and Y_L the labeled claims. The latent variables noted θ are: H_s, the probability that source s makes an honest, accurate claim c and D_m, the probability source s knows the true claim in the mutual exclusive set m for a given data item and given the observed probability $b_{s,c}$ of the claim c asserted by the source s as represented in LCA plate diagram of Figure 3.6.

The main difference with MLE is that LCA models consider the honesty of the sources. Four LCA variants have been originally proposed to capture the scenarios where the source

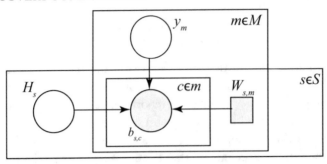

Figure 3.6: Plate diagram of SimpleLCA from Pasternack and Roth [2013].

can honestly claim some data, but sources may also guess (GUESSLCA model), do some non-intentional mistakes (MISTAKELCA model) or they can lie (LIELCA model). LCA models consider that the source truthworthiness incorporates the probability of the source being honest, knowing and telling the truth for a given data item. LCA algorithms require W, a confidence matrix that expresses the confidence of each source s in its assertions for every mutual exclusive set m (noted $w_{s,m}$ in the diagram). Typically, $w_{s,m}$ equals 1 if the source s asserts with full certainty a value for m, or 0 if the source says nothing about m.

SIMPLELCA is the simplest and most straightforward approach where each source has a probability of being honest and all sources are considered to be independent. In the Expectation step of Algorithm 3.3.2, SIMPLELCA iteratively computes the confidence of each value with β_1, the prior truth probability of the claimed value (similarly to MLE and we will see LTM). Then SIMPLELCA iteratively computes the source truthworthiness in the Maximization step, in the same way as TRUTHFINDER, averaging the confidence of the values that the source provides weighted by the certainty of the source on each of its assertions.

GUESSLCA extends SIMPLELCA with the probability of a source guessing when being honest, noted p_{g_v}. GUESSLCA rewards hard claims with correct truth label and penalizes getting easy claims wrong. It also assumes that no source will do worse than guessing, which is a significant advantage over other methods for pessimistic scenarios.

Latent Truth Model

Latent Truth Model (LTM) proposed by Zhao et al. [2012] models the probability of each claim being true as a latent Boolean random variable. Similarly to MLE and LCA, the LTM model searches for the MAP estimate but it uses collapsed Gibbs sampling. LTM has two important assumptions on the format of the data sets it can handle: (1) the data set should contain only mono-valued attributes (i.e., atomic values) and (2) LTM can handle multiple true values for the same data item. However, LTM requires the transformation of the input multi-valued claims into mono-valued claims: for ex-

Algorithm 3.3.2: SIMPLELCA(S, D, V, W, β_1, K)

Initialization. $\forall s \in S : T_S \leftarrow .8$
repeat
  $K-$
  for each $d \in D$
  Expectation step:

$$
\begin{cases}
C_{d_{sum}} \leftarrow 0 \\
\textbf{for each } v \in V_d \\
\quad \textbf{do} \begin{cases} C_v \leftarrow \beta_1. \prod_{s \in S_v} T_s^{w_{s,d}} \cdot \prod_{s' \in S_{\bar{v}}} ((1 - T_{s'})/(|V_d| - 1))^{w_{s,d}} \\[2mm] C_{d_{sum}} \leftarrow C_{d_{sum}} + C_v \end{cases} \\
\textbf{for each } v \in V_d \\
\quad \textbf{do } C_v \leftarrow C_v/C_{d_{sum}} \quad (2)
\end{cases}
$$

  Maximixation step:
  for each $s \in S_v$
    do $T_s \leftarrow \sum_{v \in V_s} C_v.w_{s,d} / \sum_{d \in D} w_{s,d}$
until $K = 0$
for each $d \in D : trueValue(d) \leftarrow \underset{v \in V_d}{\mathrm{argmax}}(C_v)$

---

ample, the claim (S1,USA.Last3Presidents,Obama, Bush,Clinton) has to be transformed into the three atomic claims (S1,USA.Last3Presidents,Obama), (S1,USA.Last3Presidents,Bush) and (S1,USA.Last3Presidents,Clinton).

LTM considers, for each source, its prior probability of true positive and negative errors, noted $\alpha_1 = (\alpha_{1,1}, \alpha_{1,0})$ as source sensitivity, as well as its prior probability of false positive and negative errors, noted $\alpha_0 = (\alpha_{0,1}, \alpha_{0,0})$ as source specificity. These priors are comparable to a and b defined in LCA models. Finally, values with confidence higher than .5 are considered to be true, thus, for some data item, LTM may not detect any true value.

LTM plate diagram is given in Figure 3.7 where each source is characterized by its false positive rate noted Φ^0 and sensitivity noted Φ^1 respectively dependent on the prior false positive and prior true negative counts (noted α_0) and the prior true positive and prior false negative counts (noted α_1). The truth label of a claim depends on the prior false (β_0) and true (β_1) count noted as $\beta = (\beta_0, \beta_1)$ in the diagram. K is the number of iterations and *burnin* and *thin* the parameters of Gibbs sampling. In practice, nine parameters need to be carefully set to execute LTM.

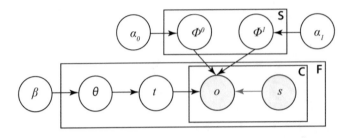

Figure 3.7: Plate diagram of LTM from Zhao et al. [2012].

In Algorithm 3.3.3, LTM maintains four counters for each source, noted n_{s,t_v,o_v}, where t_v is the Boolean truth label for each value v, and o_v is whether value v is actually claimed by the source or not. LTM first initializes the label of each claim randomly and updates the counters of each source. In each iteration, LTM samples each truth label from its distribution conditioned on all other truth labels, and the source counters are updated accordingly. In the Gibbs sampling process with K iterations, the sample size is defined as $(K - burnin)/thin$. Then LTM updates the values truth probability by discarding the first set of samples (*burnin* parameter) and, for every n samples in the remainder (*thin*), LTM computes the average to prevent correlation between adjacent samples. Finally, all values with truth probability (C_v) greater than the threshold of 0.5, are considered true, otherwise false. Since LTM relies on the random initialization of the truth labels and random sampling, multiple runs (> 100) are necessary to avoid fluctuating results with wide standard deviations. LTM does not compute source truthworthiness which gives LTM an advantage in terms of execution time.

3.3.3 ANALYTICAL METHODS

Yin and Tan [2011] propose SSTF (Semi-Supervised Truth Finder), a semi-supervised approach that learns from ground truth labeled data. The approach is based on three principles: (1) claims provided by the same data source should have similar confidence scores; (2) similar (and therefore mutually supportive) claims should have similar confidence scores; and (3) if two claims are conflicting, they cannot both be true. These three principles are encoded into a graph with claims as nodes. Relationships between claims are encoded as graph edges. If claims f_i and f_j are provided by the same data source, then edge weight w_{ij} is set to a positive value ($0 < \alpha < 1$); if f_i has a high (or low) confidence score, f_j should probably have that as well. If f_i and f_j refer to the same real-world object/attribute, then $w_{ij} = sim(f_i, f_j)$, otherwise $w_{ij} = 0$. Here, $sim(f_i, f_j)$ is a symmetric similarity function which indicates the consistency or conflict between the claims f_i and f_j with $-1 \leq sim(f_i, f_j) \leq 1$. The weight matrix $W = [w_{ij}]$ is split into four block as

Algorithm 3.3.3: $\text{LTM}(S, D, V, K, burnin, thin, \alpha_{11}, \alpha_{01}, \alpha_{00}, \alpha_{10}, \beta_0, \beta_1)$

Initialization.

for each $d \in D$

  do for each $v \in V_d$

    do $\begin{cases} C_v \leftarrow 0 \\ \textbf{if } random() < 0.5 \textbf{ then } t_v \leftarrow 0 \textbf{ else } t_v \leftarrow 1 \\ \forall s \in S_v : n_{s,t_v,o_v} \leftarrow n_{s,t_v,o_v} + 1 \\ \forall s \in S_{\bar{v}} : n_{s,t_v,o_v} \leftarrow n_{s,t_v,o_v} + 1 \end{cases}$

Sampling:

for $i \leftarrow 1$ **to** K

do $\begin{cases} i \leftarrow i + 1 \\ \textbf{for each } d \in D \\ \quad \textbf{do for each } v \in V_d \\ \qquad \textbf{do} \begin{cases} p_{t_v} \leftarrow \beta_{t_v}; p_{t_{\bar{v}}} \leftarrow \beta_{t_{\bar{v}}} \\ \textbf{for each } s \in S_v \cup S_{\bar{v}} \\ \quad \textbf{do} \begin{cases} p_{t_v} \leftarrow \dfrac{p_{t_v}(n_{s,t_v,o_v}+\alpha_{t_v,o_v}-1)}{n_{s,t_v,1}+n_{s,t_v,0}+\alpha_{t_v,1}+\alpha_{t_v,0}-1} \\[2ex] p_{t_{\bar{v}}} \leftarrow \dfrac{p_{t_{\bar{v}}}(n_{s,t_{\bar{v}},o_v}+\alpha_{t_{\bar{v}},o_v}-1)}{n_{s,t_{\bar{v}},1}+n_{s,t_{\bar{v}},0}+\alpha_{t_{\bar{v}},1}+\alpha_{t_{\bar{v}},0}} \end{cases} \\ \textbf{if } random() < \dfrac{p_{t_{\bar{v}}}}{p_{t_v}+p_{t_{\bar{v}}}} \\ \quad \textbf{then} \begin{cases} t_v \leftarrow 1 - t_v \\ \textbf{for each } s \in S_v \cup S_{\bar{v}} \\ \quad \textbf{do} \begin{cases} n_{s,t_{\bar{v}},o_v} \leftarrow n_{s,t_{\bar{v}},o_v} - 1 \\ n_{s,t_v,o_v} \leftarrow n_{s,t_v,o_v} + 1 \end{cases} \end{cases} \\ \textbf{if } i > burnin \& i\%thin = 0 \\ \quad \textbf{then } C_v \leftarrow C_v + \dfrac{t_v.thin}{(K-burnin)} \end{cases} \end{cases}$

for each $d \in D$

  for each $v \in V_d$

    If $C_v > 0.5$ **then** $trueValue(d) \leftarrow v$

$W = \begin{bmatrix} W_{LL} & W_{LU} \\ W_{UL} & W_{UU} \end{bmatrix}$ of edges from labeled (L) or unlabeled (U) to labeled/unlabeled nodes. SSTF then learns a confidence value between -1 and 1 for each claim. Truth discovery is equivalent to solving an graph optimization problem that aims to assign scores to the graph nodes that are consistent with the relationships indicated by the graph edges. Specifically, the objective function to be minimized is

$$E(c) = \frac{1}{2} \sum_{i,j} |w_{ij}| (c_i - s_{ij} c_j)^2 \tag{3.3}$$

where $s_{ij} = 1$ if $w_{ij} \geq 0$ for supportive claims and -1 if $w_{ij} < 0$ for conflicting claims. So as to find the score c^* such as:

$$\left. \frac{\partial E(c)}{\partial c} \right|_{c=c^*} \tag{3.4}$$

The authors provide an efficient analytical solution to this optimization problem based on matrix diagonalization in such a way that the previous equation is rewritten as:

$$\left. \frac{\partial E(c)}{\partial c} \right|_{c=c^*} \Leftrightarrow (D_{UU} - W_{UU})C_U - W_{UL}C_L = 0 \tag{3.5}$$

where the edge weights from similar unlabeled data (W_{UU} from the weight matrix) to labeled data (W_{UL}) should have similar confidence scores and D_{UU} is the diagonal matrix from the weight matrix W_{UU} of the unlabeled claims as $D_{ii} = \sum_j |w_{ij}|$.

For relatively large datasets (e.g., 49M facts, 65.7M objects, 89M data sources in the experiments reported in Yin and Tan [2011]), SSTF converges with a steady pace and is not sensitive to changes in parameter values. The authors varied the size of the training set and conclude that SSTF can significantly improve accuracy with a small training set and is significantly faster than many other approaches. They also tested the scalability of their approach on synthetic datasets and observe close to linear increase in time required and memory consumed as the number of claims is increased.

3.3.4   BAYESIAN INFERENCE-BASED METHODS

Source Dependence in Truth Discovery
DEPEN proposed by Dong et al. [2009a] and further extended in Dong et al. [2009b, 2010b] is the first Bayesian truth detection model that takes into consideration the copying relationships between sources. It is based on the underlying intuition that sharing the same errors is unlikely if sources are independent. Formalizing this principle, DEPEN penalizes the vote count of a source if the source is detected to be a copier of another source. DEPEN is presented with four extensions in its original paper [Dong et al., 2009a]; in particular, ACCU relaxes the assumption that the sources have the same probability of providing a true value and ACCUSIM extends ACCU to take

into account value similarity. In these models, the source accuracy is computed such as:

$$A(S) = Avg_{v(d) \in S}\left(Pr(v(d) \ \texttt{IsTrue}|\Phi)\right) \qquad (3.6)$$

where S provides value v on data item d, $v(d) \in S$; the observations on all data items covered by sources in S are considered, Φ; and $Pr(v(d) \ \texttt{IsTrue}|\Phi)$ is the probability of $v(d)$ being true.

Algorithm 3.3.4: DEPEN$(S, D, V, n, c, \alpha, \delta)$

Initialization.
$\forall s \in S : T_s \leftarrow 0.8$
$\forall d \in D : trueValue(d) \leftarrow \text{argmax}_{v \in V_d}(|S_v|)$
$\forall s_i \in S, \forall s_j \in S - \{s_i\} : CompDepen(s_i, s_j, \alpha, n)$
repeat
 for each $d \in D$
  do for each $v \in V_d$

$$\textbf{do} \begin{cases} O_{S_v} \leftarrow orderByDepen(S_v) \\ Pre \leftarrow \emptyset; C_v \leftarrow 0; t_{scores} \leftarrow 1; \\ \textbf{for each } s \in O_{S_v} \\ \quad \textbf{do} \begin{cases} \textbf{if } Pre == \emptyset \\ \quad \textbf{then } voteCount = 1 \\ \quad \textbf{else } voteCount = \prod\limits_{s_j \in Pre} (1 - (c.depen(s, s_j))) \\ addToList(Pre, s) \\ C_v \leftarrow C_v + t_{scores}.voteCount \end{cases} \end{cases}$$

 for each $s \in S_v$
  do $T_s \leftarrow \frac{1}{|V_s|} \sum\limits_{v \in V_s} \frac{e^{C_v}}{\sum\limits_{v' \in V_{D_v}} e^{C_{v'}}}$

 $\forall s_i \in S, \forall s_j \in S - \{s_i\} : CompDepen(s_i, s_j, \alpha, n)$

until $Convergence(T_s, \delta)$
for each $d \in D$
 do $trueValue(d) \leftarrow \text{argmax}(C_v)$
  $\phantom{\textbf{do} trueValue(d) \leftarrow}{}_{v \in V_d}$

In its Algorithm 3.3.4, DEPEN starts by initializing all sources' truthworthiness to .8. For every data item, it selects the true value by majority voting, and computes the dependence between sources with the function $CompDepen(s_i, s_j, \alpha, n)$ where the dependence probability between two sources s_i and s_j is defined as

$$depen(s_i, s_j) = p(s_i \longrightarrow s_j) + p(s_j \longrightarrow s_i)$$

with

$$p(s_i \longrightarrow s_j) = \frac{\alpha Dep(s_i, s_j)}{\alpha Dep(s_i, s_j) + \alpha Dep(s_j, s_i) + (1 - 2\alpha)noDep}$$

with α the *a priori* probability that s_i and s_j are dependent, and

$$\begin{cases} noDep & = p_t^{n_t} \cdot p_f^{n_f} \cdot \left(1 - p_t - p_f\right)^{n_d} \\ Dep(s_i, s_j) = \left(cT_{s_i} + p_t(1 - c)\right)^{n_t} \cdot \left(c(1 - T_{s_i}) + p_f(1 - c)\right)^{n_f} \cdot \left((1 - p_t - p_f)(1 - c)\right)^{n_d} \end{cases}$$
$$(3.7)$$

where n_t is the number of true common values between s_i and s_j; n_f is the number of false common values between s_i and s_j; n_d is the number of different values between s_i and s_j; $p_t = T_{s_i} \cdot T_{s_j}$ and $p_f = \frac{(1 - T_{s_i})(1 - T_{s_i})}{n}$, and n is the number of false values per data item.

To iteratively compute the value confidence, the sources claiming the considered value are first ordered by their dependence probabilities with *orderByDepen(S_v)* function in the algorithm. Then each source's *voteCount* is computed in a way that minimizes the vote if the source is dependent on other sources in *Pre*, the list of ranked sources, such as

$$voteCount = \prod_{s_j \in Pre} (1 - c.depen(s, s_j)),$$

with c the probability that a value provided by a copier is copied. *voteCount* is then weighted by t_{scores}, the source's score to compute the value confidence. Source truthworthiness is then computed iteratively as a function of the confidence of all values claimed by the sources. True values are expected to be the values with the highest confidence. Source dependence detection as originally proposed is very computationally expensive but a scalable version has been proposed recently by Li et al. [2015a].

In Chapter 2, we have already mentioned the Knowledge Vault project [Dong et al., 2014a] extracting about 3 billion of triples from 2.5 billion of urls (28 millions of websites) as of 2014. Interestingly this project also made use of Expectation-Maximization and Bayesian inference on a multi-layer model. Its main particularity is to distinguish between extractor errors and source errors. The model captures the error that each information extractor (16 extractors were used) may produce when extracting values from Web tables, texts, or DOM documents. The model is represented as the plate diagram of Figure 3.8 where w_{ewdv} is the observation of the value v extracted by the extractor e from a Web source w for a given data item d. This observation depends on three parameters of the model: the recall and precision of the extractor e and the accuracy A_w of the Web source; the latent variables to estimate are: v_d the correct value for data item d and c_{wdv} the variable that represents whether source w indeed provides the value v for data item d. Mainly using Bayesian inference, the system first computes the probability that a Web source provides the correct value for a data item d given the extractor quality, then it computes the probability that a value is the correct one given its source quality, then it computes the source accuracy, precision, and recall of each extractor.

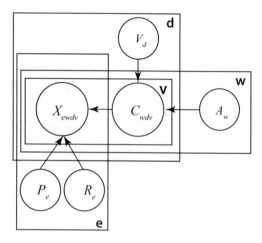

Figure 3.8: Plate diagram of knowledge fusion from Dong et al. [2014a].

3.4 NEW DEVELOPMENTS

Recent contributions have substantially improved previous approaches modeling and overcome their limitations mainly related to four aspects: the evolving truth, the cardinality of truth, the heterogeneity of source coverage (referred to as the long-tail phenomenon), and truth discovery from crowdsourced data.

3.4.1 EVOLVING TRUTH DISCOVERY

Three approaches have been proposed to capture the notion of evolving truth.

(1) First, true values can evolve over time, e.g., in a career, the affiliation of a researcher is very likely to change, so is the address of a restaurant, or the status of a flight. But sources' behavior can also change over time. The method proposed in Dong et al. [2009b] captures the lifespan of each object as well as the copying relationship between sources and computes a more complex definition of the source accuracy based on source dependence. Enhancing their previous model from Dong et al. [2009a, 2010b], they incorporate source coverage, exactness, and freshness into the computation of source accuracy. They propose the Hidden Markov model presented as a transition graph in Figure 3.9. Assuming that the source copying relationship is acyclic, at each moment there can be at most one copier between two sources S_1 and S_2. In case a particular source

is a copier, it can copy or independently update at a particular observation point. Thus, there are five hidden states: I, $C1_c$, $C1_{\neg c}$, $C2_c$, and $C2_{\neg c}$. State I represents independence of S_1 and S_2. States $C1_c$ and $C1_{\neg c}$ represent that S_1 is a copier of S_2; the former represents S_1 actively copying from S_2 and the latter represents S_1 not copying at that moment. Similarly, states $C2_c$ and $C2_{\neg c}$ represent S_2 copying or not copying while being a copier of S_1.

$C1_{\neg c}$, $C2_{\neg c}$, and I are not distinguishable from the action of S_1 and S_2: in all cases S_1 and S_2 make independent updates but their probability of transition from one of these states to state $C1_c$ (or $C2_c$) can be different (as presented in the figure): intuitively, S_1 is more likely to actively copy from S_2 (so in state $C1_c$) next when it is in state $C1_{\neg c}$ than in state I.

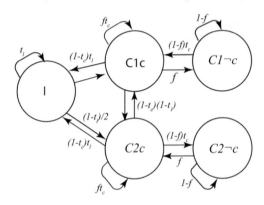

Figure 3.9: HMM capturing the transitions of the sources' behavior in their copying relationships from Dong et al. [2009b].

(2) Second, source quality may change over time, the work of Li et al. [2015b] uses MAP estimation for computing source weights in a time interval T. This approach typically minimizes a loss function l_t at time t for all the information claimed by the sources from timestamp 1 to T. All the information collected for a given object are aggregated and a weighted distance is measured between the information provided by each source and the aggregated information across all sources at a given time. This represents the error of the source s at time t for a given object o, noted $e_{o,t}^s$. This error is assumed to follow a normal distribution $e_{o,t}^s | w_s \sim N(0, \frac{1}{\theta w_s})$ where θ is the trade-off parameter of the loss function and w_s is the source weight to estimate. Constraints and prior knowledge about source weights are encoded in the method. Finally, minimizing the loss function is assumed to be equivalent to maximizing the likelihood $\prod_{s=1}^{S} p(e_{1:T}^s | w_s)$ and the authors proposed an incremental algorithm to compute the source weights.

(3) Finally, another aspect to consider for capturing evolving truth is the case when new sources or new claims are added. In the approach of Jia et al. [2013], incremental voting over multiple trained classifiers is proposed to capture this aspect as well as the data drift. Zhao et al. [2014] address the problem of truth discovery in data streams as an optimization problem and propose

a probabilistic inference model and *StreamTF*, the one-pass algorithm based on the stochastic natural gradient [Bottou, 1998] that computes the source quality and true values in real time.

3.4.2 ZERO-TO-MANY TRUTH

The cardinality of truth is another important aspect to consider for improving the modeling and capturing more realistic truth discovery scenarios. Previous approaches only assume that one and usually only one value for each data item is true. However, no-truth cases exist where none of the values provided by the sources are true. On the other hand, multiple true values are also possible.

In the TEM (Truth Existence Model) proposed by Zhi et al. [2015] and represented as Plate diagram in Figure 3.10, source quality is revisited in order to integrate three measures: source silent rate, false spoken rate, and true spoken rate as the priors (noted α) of source quality (noted Φ) in the diagram. The N sources are assumed to be mutually independent. The true value among the claims A depends on the truth prior η. The authors use Expectation Maximization to infer jointly truth and source quality although no truth may exist.

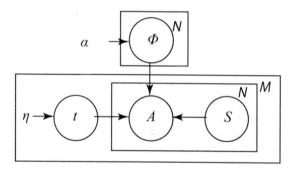

Figure 3.10: Plate diagram of TEM model from Zhi et al. [2015].

The work of Wang et al. [2015b] addresses the problem of multi-truth discovery for the case of multi-valued data items (i.e., lists). Sometimes lists of values claimed by multiple sources may overlap and claiming one value for a data item does not necessarily imply disclaiming all the other values for this particular data item. This case where the claimed value may only cover the truth partially has been addressed in Wang et al. [2015b]. The approach called MTF (Multi-Truth Finding) is a Bayesian model that incorporates source and value grouping, source dependency inference, and inter-value mutual exclusion.

The same authors in Wang et al. [2015a] have leveraged and enhanced their grouping technique to improve truth discovery efficiency via problem scale reduction. They propose content-based and mapping-based grouping methods to reduce the size of the sources' and the values' sets, respectively. Ultimately, the user can specify the trade-off between efficiency and accuracy. Their method then recommends the group of values with the highest veracity score as the approximate truth.

3.4.3   LONG-TAIL PHENOMENON

Consider the extreme case when most sources only make one claim to one single item. If the claim is correct, source accuracy equals 1 and the sources are considered highly reliable. If the claim is wrong, source accuracy is null and the sources are regarded as highly unreliable. When weighted voting is conducted based on traditional estimates of source reliability, this estimation of the source reliability is biased for many sources with small coverage and it will inevitably impair the ability of detecting trustworthy information. This problem known as the *long-tail phenomenon* has been addressed by Li et al. [2014] who proposed the confidence-aware truth discovery (CATD) method. This method computes the source weight as a function inversely proportional to the upper bound of the $(1 - \alpha)$ confidence interval for its real variance (for $\alpha = .05$). The variance of the error distribution of the source s noted σ_s^2 actually reflects the reliability of s. In this approach, none of the sources is considered to make errors on purpose and each source has an error that follows a Gaussian distribution such as $\epsilon_s = N(0, \sigma^2)$. The source weight is computed based on the Chi-squared probability value which will dominate the weight when a source provides only few claims and on the other hand, if a source provides a sufficient number of claims, and the chi-squared probability is close to $|V_s|$ and has a small bias on the estimator.

3.4.4   TRUTH DISCOVERY FROM CROWDSOURCED DATA

In the context of human sensing, recent contributions investigate the potential of leveraging crowds to report events [Ma et al., 2015] or quantitative information [Ouyang et al., 2015]. There exist many conflicts in the answers provided by the crowd participants and one challenge is in aggregating crowdsourced data because the reliability or expertise of the source may depend on the topic or the question. To address this problem, a fairly complex model, FAITCROWD (Fine Grained Truth Discovery model for Crowd) illustrated in Figure 3.11 has been proposed by Ma et al. [2015]. It takes as inputs: Q questions, K topics, M_q words and N_q answers per question provided by U users, and eight prior parameters of the model and it returns the user's expertise e, the true answers t_q, and the question topic labels z_q. The authors employ a hybrid inference method combining sampling and the variational optimization Gibbs-EM [Wallach, 2006]. According to the authors, the method is not affected by parameter settings and has linear time with the number of answers.

Ouyang et al. [2015] investigate how accurately each crowd participant can estimate quantitative information such as counts or percentages and whether there exist bias and variance in their estimates. The Truth Bias and Precision (TBP) model illustrated as a Plate diagram in Figure 3.12 considers latent quantitative truths (z_j), underlying task difficulties (r_j), crowd participants' biases (h_{ik}), and precisions (λ_{ik}) in the quantity estimation from the crowdsourced claims (x_{ij}). The underlying difficulty of a task impacts which bias and precision parameters a crowd participant will use to generate a claim. The authors proposed batch and online inference based on Expectation-Maximization and minimum mean squared error (MMSE) respectively.

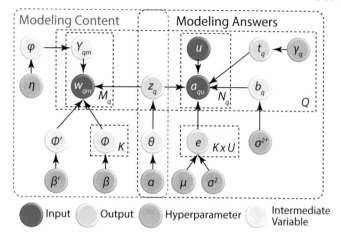

Figure 3.11: Plate diagram of FAITCROWD from Ma et al. [2015].

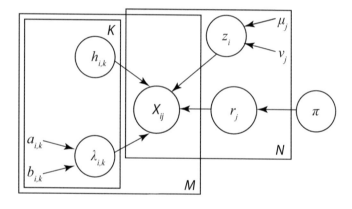

Figure 3.12: Plate diagram of TBP from Ouyang et al. [2015].

3.5   CONCLUSION

There are a number of challenges in truth discovery from structured data. The first challenge is a conceptual one since it is difficult to define a method or a model general enough to handle various data set characteristics and a large spectrum of truth discovery scenarios. We can observe that none of the methods constantly outperforms the others in terms of precision/recall and a "one-size-fits-all" approach does not seem to be achievable. Most of the current methods have been designed for excelling in *optimistic* scenarios with a reasonable number of honest and reliable sources. However, experiments reported in Waguih and Berti-Equille [2014] revealed that, for *pessimistic* or adversarial scenarios when most sources are not reliable, most of the methods have relatively low precision, some expose prohibitive runtime and may suffer from scalability or fluctuating results.

Another challenge is related to the usability of the methods. The assumptions made by current truth discovery models and their complex parameter setting make them still difficult to be actionable and applied to the wide diversity of information and scenarios available on the Web. Since limited ground truth is available but is usually not statistically significant, the performance evaluation and comparative study of the methods is a very difficult task and benchmarks are critically needed. Although recent contributions address the scalability issues [Dong et al., 2014b, Li et al., 2015a, Wang et al., 2015a] and some others relax some of the modeling assumptions of the previous work, truth discovery remains a long-standing problem far from being solved and our view (which actually motivated this book) is that it requires a transdisciplinary approach to properly incorporate two of its intrinsic dimensions related to dynamics and complex networks of sources and content.

CHAPTER 4

Trust Computation

4.1 INTRODUCTION

Truth discovery from the Web has significant practical importance: online rumor propagation [Kwon et al., 2013], mis- or disinformation can have tremendous impacts on our society, economy, politics, and homeland security. For example, the *Fog Computing* project from DARPA is a prototype developed in response to Wikileaks for automatically generating and distributing believable misinformation and then tracking access and attempted misuse of the *Fog Computing* project.[1]. Online fact-checkers such as FactCheck,[2] Snopes,[3] PolitiFact,[4] TruthorFiction,[5] or OpenSecrets[6]) have gained unprecedented attention since their goal is to classify and verify manually (or semi-automatically) online information for public opinion.

From this online fact-checking and computational journalism [Cohen et al., 2011a, Hassan et al., 2015], the problem of truth discovery is closely related to the notion of trust. We can trust a source although it may provide sometimes false information. So the distinction between trustworthiness, trust, and truth has to be made and it actually motivated this chapter. Trustworthiness and reputation of the sources is critical in estimating information credibility. Trust management has been extensively studied in many contexts and equally diverse domains such as human social networks, E-commerce, mobile ad-hoc networks, peer-to-peer networks, etc. In this chapter, we will review the field of trust management, starting with the definitions of its core concepts and surveying the main models for computing direct and indirect trust and modeling trust propagation.

4.2 DEFINITIONS

A commonly accepted definition of **Trust** has been proposed by Gambetta [1988] as: "a particular level of the subjective probability with which an agent will perform a particular action, both before [we] can monitor such action [...] and in a context in which it affects [our] own action."

From this probabilistic definition, three properties of trust have emerged: subjectiveness, context-dependence, and dynamic behavior. The same behavior may lead to different trust levels due to the subjective appreciations of different trusting entities. The context of appreciation may

---

[1]Fog Computing project http://www.dtic.mil/dtic/tr/fulltext/u2/a552461.pdf
[2]FactCheck, http://www.factcheck.org/
[3]Snopes, http://www.snopes.com/
[4]PolitiFact,http://www.politifact.com/
[5]TruthorFiction, http://www.truthorfiction.com/
[6]OpenSecrets, http://www.opensecrets.org/

also change the level of trust. More formally, the concept of trust, in the case of two parties involved in an evolving trust relationship can be defined such that an entity, the *trustor* T_R, is considered to trust another entity T_E, the *trustee*, when T_R believes that entity T_E will behave exactly as expected and required. The trustor must decide whether and how much to trust the trustee based on an assessment of its historical experience and the trustee's reputation rather than a blind guess.

Trustworthiness is the objective probability that the trustee performs a particular action on which the interests of the trustor depend.

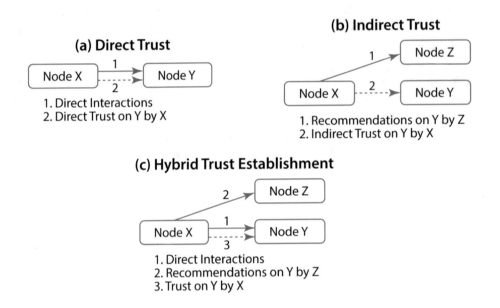

Figure 4.1: Main trust computing schemes.

Reputation relates to trust, as the following definition from Mui et al. [2001]: "Reputation is perception that an agent creates through past actions about its intentions and norms." Actions build up reputation (the perception about intentions and norms). Direct experiences and recommendations about one entity describe the entity's past actions, which, thus, create the entity's reputation.

Trust purpose defines the specific scope of a given trust relationship. The survey of Jøsang and Haller [2007] describes different trust classes and categories for reputation and trust semantics, and provides a good overview of various trust management and reputation systems.

Trust degree indicates the trustworthy level of a certain entity. It is usually computed as the weighted average of direct and indirect trust degrees. Direct trust degree is updated according to each history-based behavior and experience of the trustee entity in a given context. Indirect trust degree also referred to as reputation can be associated with other evidence not included in a trustor's direct experience. It is related to recommendations from other evaluation entities.

These notions are illustrated in Figure 4.1 where the three main types of trust computing schemes have been proposed [Govindan and Mohapatra, 2012, Jøsang et al., 2007, Momani, 2010, Thirunarayan et al., 2014]: (a) direct trust computation based on neighboring entities, (b) indirect trust computation based on recommendation, and (c) hybrid schema combining direct and indirect trust computation.

In the next section, we will detail the methods for each type of trust computing schema with its theoretical underpinning.

4.3 PROBABILISTIC TRUST COMPUTATION

There are many computational models of trust, a review of which can be found in Ramchurn et al. [2004]. Bayesian statistics provides a theoretical foundation for measuring the uncertainty in a decision that is based on a collection of observations. The principle of trust evaluation consists in knowing the distribution of satisfaction levels from each node involved in a trust relationship and using this information to estimate the satisfaction level of future consultations. For the case of a binary satisfaction level (satisfied, not satisfied), a Beta distribution can be used as proposed by Ganeriwal et al. [2008]. For multi-valued satisfaction levels, Dirichlet distributions are more appropriate for direct trust estimation as we will describe in the next sections dedicated to direct trust models.

4.3.1 DIRECT TRUST MODELS

Beta PDF for Bi-valued Trust Metric

The Beta probability density distribution is based on initial beliefs about an unknown event represented as a prior distribution. The initial beliefs combined with collected sample data can be represented as a posterior distribution. The posterior distribution well suits many trust management models since the trust is updated based on the interaction history.

Bayesian systems take binary ratings as input (i.e., positive or negative), and compute reputation scores by statistically updating the Beta probability density functions (PDF). The *a posteriori* (i.e., the updated) reputation score is computed by combining the *a priori* (i.e., previous) reputation score with the new rating. The reputation score can be represented in the form of the Beta PDF parameter tuple (α, β) where α and β represent the amount of positive and negative ratings respectively, or in the form of the probability expectation value of the Beta PDF, eventually with the variance or a confidence parameter. The Beta PDF denoted by $Beta(p|\alpha, \beta)$ can be expressed using the Γ function[7] as:

$$Beta(p|\alpha, \beta) = \frac{\Gamma(\alpha + \beta)}{\Gamma(\alpha)\Gamma(\beta)} p^{\alpha-1}(1 - p)^{\beta-1} \qquad (4.1)$$

[7]https://en.wikipedia.org/wiki/Gamma_function

where $0 \leq p \leq 1$, $\alpha, \beta > 0$, with the restriction that the probability variable $p \neq 0$ if $\alpha < 1$, and $p \neq 1$ if $\beta < 1$. The probability expectation value of the Beta distribution is:

$$E(p) = \frac{\alpha}{\alpha + \beta} \qquad (4.2)$$

Equation 4.2 represents the overall reputation from the total number of supportive observations (s) and the total number of opposing observations (r) collected so far. When nothing is known, the a priori distribution is the uniform Beta PDF with $\alpha = 1$ and $\beta = 1$. Then, after observing r positive and s negative outcomes, the a posteriori distribution is the Beta PDF with $\alpha = r + 1$ and $\beta = s + 1$ with $r, s \geq 0$. This PDF expresses the uncertain probability that future interactions will be positive. As proposed by Jøsang and Ismail [2002], a way to define the reputation score is as a function of the expectation value. In the field of computational trust, there are a couple of Beta distribution-based reputation models. In particular, the Beta Reputation System [Jøsang and Ismail, 2002] is a centralized probabilistic trust model designed for online communities. It works by users giving ratings to the performance of other users in the community. Ratings consist of a single value that is used to obtain positive and negative feedback values. The feedback values are then used to calculate distribution shape parameters that determine the reputation of the user the rating is applied to.

Example 4.1   For example, the Beta PDF after observing seven positive and one negative outcomes is illustrated in Figure 4.2. The probability expectation value according to Eq. (4.2) can be interpreted such that the relative frequency of a positive outcome in the future is somewhat uncertain, and the most likely value is $E(p) = 8/10 = .8$.

Dirichlet PDF for Multi-valued Trust Metric

The multinomial distribution is a generalization of the binomial for the situation in which we deal with several categories of observations, as opposed to just two (e.g., positive/negative). Multinomial distribution is particularly adapted when multiple ratings or levels are available for trust computation and it has been used in various applications of computational trust. For example, [Thirunarayan et al., 2014] provide the method of Dirichlet distribution for direct trust computation and trust evolution in response to different behaviors in reputation systems. Yang and Cemerlic [2009] discuss the approach of Dirichlet distribution to compute reputation to minimize risk in usage control in a collaborative environment. Jøsang et al. [2007] use Dirichlet distribution for their multi-level reputation system in the context of e-commence. Fung et al. [2011] also use Dirichlet distribution for trust management to collaborative host-based intrusion detection networks to improve security.

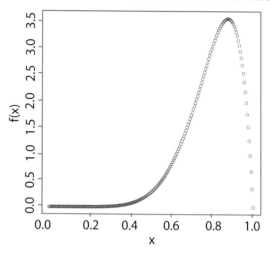

Figure 4.2: Example of Beta probability density function with $\alpha = 8$ and $\beta = 2$.

Let $y = (y_1, \ldots, y_k)$ the number of independent observations that results in k trust levels $i = 1, \ldots, k$. The likelihood function noted $f(y|p)$ is

$$f(y|p) \propto \prod_{i=1}^{k} p_i^{y_i} \qquad (4.3)$$

where p_i is the probability that a given observation belongs to one of k category.

The Dirichlet PDF is

$$Dirichlet(p|\alpha) = \frac{1}{B(\alpha)} \prod_{i=1}^{k} p_i^{\alpha_i - 1} \qquad (4.4)$$

where $p_i \geq 0$, $\sum_{i=1}^{k} p_i = 1$ and $\alpha_i > 0$. The parameter α_i can be interpreted as prior observation counts for the events of category i. The normalization constant $B(\alpha)$ is

$$B(\alpha) = \prod_{i=1}^{k} \Gamma(\alpha_i) / \Gamma(\sum_{i=1}^{k} \alpha_i)$$

that is the multinomial generalization of Beta density probability function.

Using α_i as the prior in the above multinomial case yields a Dirichlet posterior with parameters $y_i + \alpha_i$. The probability density function of posterior distribution is

$$Dirichlet(p|y + \alpha) = \frac{1}{B(y + \alpha)} \prod_{i=1}^{k} p_i^{y_i + \alpha_i - 1} \qquad (4.5)$$

The expected value of each probability p_i in the Dirichlet distribution is the relative frequency for occurrences of events in the category i defined as

$$E(p_i) = \frac{\alpha_i}{\sum_{j=1}^{k} \alpha_j} \tag{4.6}$$

The expected value can be interpreted as the chance of an event of category i occurring in the next observation. So, if there is an experiment with observation parameter x, the posterior distribution with non-informative prior with $\alpha_i = 1$ can be modeled as $Dirichlet(p|x + 1)$ and the chance of an event of category i occurring in next observation, becomes

$$E(p_i) = \frac{x_i + 1}{k + \sum_{i=1}^{k} x_i} \tag{4.7}$$

In the case of Beta distribution, that we have only two categories and events of each category has occurred x_1 and x_2 times respectively, the expected value for p_1 becomes $\frac{x_1+1}{x_1+x_2+2}$.

Example 4.2   Consider two nodes A and B interacting with each other. A had five positive and two negative observations from its past experiences with B. In this situation, the probability that B acts positively in the next interaction with A according to Eq. (4.7) is equal to the expected value of p_1 in Dirichlet distribution with posterior $Dirichlet(p; [5 + 1, 2 + 1])$, so it results in $E(p_1) = 6/9$. Similarly the probability that B acts negatively with respect to A is $E(p_2) = 3/9$.

Example 4.3   Suppose now that the quality of experiences in the previous example is divided into three levels: good, average, and bad. And there are 4, 1, and 2 observations for good, average, and bad experiences respectively. So the probability that B acts in a positive manner with A can be calculated from the expected value of p_1 based on $Dirichlet(p; [5, 2, 3])$ that is $E(p_{good}) = (4 + 1)/(4 + 1 + 2 + 3) = 5/10$. Likewise the probability of being average and bad will be 2/10 and 3/10 respectively.

4.3.2   COMBINING DIRECT AND INDIRECT TRUST MODELS

Direct observation cannot always be possible for inferring the trustworthiness of an entity. Thus, referrals are commonly used for estimating indirectly the trustworthiness. In practice, trust assessment in the Web combines both approaches of direct trust based on direct experience for Web sites that are often visited, and inferred trust based on referrals for occasionally visited sites. The effectiveness of the latter depends on the accuracy of the referrals and the trust inference method for estimating trust propagation. A large body of research has focused on trust metrics, trust modeling, and inference in Semantic Web applications, recommender systems, and other contexts such as ad hoc networks and peer-to-peer systems. The proposed approaches can classified be into four categories.

- Based on an aggregation function: e.g., sum of positive/negative ratings (e.g., eBay reputation forum[8]).

- Based on linear algebra applied to Markovian models: trust inference is based on a probabilistic interpretation of the transition from host to host, e.g., Gyöngyi et al. [2004].

- Based on path algebra: the trust network is modeled as a directed-weighted graph; the weight of each edge connecting two nodes equals the value of the direct trust, while end-to-end trust of some path is inferred by calculating the weight of the path, e.g., Golbeck et al. [2003].

- Other specialized approaches: e.g., those involving multi-dimensional trust metrics [Jøsang and Pope, 2005].

Various trust metrics have been proposed for each type of approach. Other measures from information theory have been used to estimate the uncertainty of the recommendations. In Sun et al. [2006b], a trust score T in $[-1,1]$ represents the degree of trust that an opinion or a recommendation provided by member u to member d will help to make appropriate decisions. On Twitter, a trust score is assigned for each pair of social network members (d,u) whenever d *follows u*. $P(u)$ denotes the probability that u provides a recommendation such as $P(u) = (k + 1)/(n + 2)$ with k, the number of friends of member u that are part of the relationship requests (some members want to follow u), and n, the total number of relationship requests. Then the trust score T is computed based on the entropy $H(P(u)) = P(u) \log_2 P(u) - (1 - P(u)) \log_2(1 - P(u))$ as follows:

$$T = \begin{cases} 1 - H(P(u)), \text{for } 0.5 \le P(u) \le 1 \\ H(P(u)) - 1, \text{for } 0 \le P(u) < 0.5 \end{cases}$$

The trust score will be negative for $0 \le P(u) < 0.5$, indicating distrust, or positive for $0.5 \le P(u) \le 1$ indicating trust.

In Ganeriwal et al. [2008] applied to sensor networks, the (α, β) parameters associated with the Beta PDF can be obtained from success experiences s and failure experiences f such as:

$$(\alpha, \beta) = (s + 1, f + 1).(s_j^{new}, f_j^{new})$$

The values to compute trust of trustor i in trustee j are obtained by combining the direct experiences (s_j, f_j) by trustor i with trustee j, and the indirect experiences (s_j^k, f_j^k) by node k with trustee j weighted by (s_k, f_k) the direct experiences by trustor i with node k, using the chaining/discounting rule given in Sun et al. [2006b] as

$$\begin{cases} \alpha_j^{new} = \alpha_j + \dfrac{2\alpha_k \alpha_j^k}{(\beta_k + 2)(\beta_j^k + \beta_j^k + 2) + 2\alpha_k} \\ \beta_j^{new} = \beta_j + \dfrac{2\alpha_k \beta_j^k}{(\beta_k + 2)(\beta_j^k + \beta_j^k + 2) + 2\alpha_k} \end{cases} \qquad (4.8)$$

[8]eBay, http://www.e-bay.com

In Denko-Sun's approach for MANETs [Denko and Sun, 2008], direct trust in a trustee by a trustor is based on the number of success experiences s and the number of failure experiences f witnessed by the trustor, and indirect trust is obtained via recommendations from k nodes and is based on the total number of success experiences s^r and the total number of failure experiences f^r reported by the recommender. Cumulative trust T is obtained by summing both direct and indirect counts such as:

$$T = (s + s^r + 1)/((s + s^r + 1) + (f + f^r + 1))$$

where $s^r = \sum_{i=1}^{k} s_i^r$ and $f^r = \sum_{i=1}^{k} f_i^r$. Each node maintains, for each peer (and for the implicit context of packet forwarding), these numbers.

4.3.3   EVALUATION OF TRUST COMPUTING SCHEMES

Possible attacks are used for comparing trust computing schemes. The ones presented in Table 4.1 have been identified in mobile ad-hoc networks (MANETs) and classified by Govindan and Mohapatra [2012].

Table 4.1: Attack schemes in trust computation from Govindan and Mohapatra [2012]

Attack Type	Description
Denial of service attack (DOS)	The attackers send as much trust recommendations as possible to consume the large amount of computing resources in the trust calculating nodes.
Bad mouthing attack (BMA)	A node gives bad recommendation intentionally about other nodes.
On-off attack (OOA)	Malicious entities can opportunistically behave good and bad as per the importance of situation.
Conflicting behavior attack (CBA)	Malicious entities provide conflicting recommendations to different groups of nodes to create confusion in trust evaluation.
Sybil attack (SA)	A malicious node will create several fake IDs.
Camouflage attack (CA)	The dishonest nodes attempt to build up trust by always reporting as per the observed majority. After they earn enough trust values, they behave dishonestly only for specific occasions.
Collusion attack (CoA)	More than one collaborating malicious node gives false recommendations about normal nodes.
Newcomer attacks (NCA)	The attacker simply leaves the system and joins again hoping to flush out the previous bad history and to accumulate new trust [Resnick et al., 2000].

4.4   TRUST PROPAGATION

The advantage of having a platform where users provide information about their trust connection to other users is the possibility to use that information to infer additional trust connections by means of trust propagation. Taking users as nodes and trust statements as edges, a trust graph can be inferred, often referred to as Web of Trust.

There are many approaches in the literature that present trust computation and formalize trust propagation either along chained paths, trust aggregation from multiple sources, or overriding (e.g., Guha et al. [2004]).

4.4.1   OVERRIDING TRUST PROPAGATION

Guha and colleagues [Guha et al., 2004] developed a framework to propagate trust in a Web of Trust with the goal to "predict an unknown trust/distrust value between any two users" based on existing trust and distrust information. In the framework, for a universe of n users, there are two global matrices storing trust and distrust. The trust matrix T as $t_{ij} \in [0, 1]$ entries meaning that user i trusts j with value t_{ij}. Analogously, the distrust matrix D has $d_{ij} \in [0, 1]$ entries expressing the distrust between user i and user j. The propagation of trust and distrust starts with a generic belief matrix B, which is based on T and D. The specific way in which B is composed can differ depending on the implementation and desired propagation behavior of mistrust. There are four different basic propagation techniques, referred to as atomic propagation steps (see Table 4.2).

Table 4.2: Trust propagation operations

Propagation	Operator	Description
Direct	B	If A trusts B, someone trusted by B should also be trusted by A.
Co-citation	$B^T.B$	If A trusts B and C, someone trusting C should also trust B.
Transpose Trust	B^T	If A trusts B, someone trusting B should also trust A.
Coupling	$B.B^T$	If A and B trusts C, someone trusting A should also trust B.

Distrust is not necessarily transitive. If A does not trust B and B does not trust C, it is not clear whether A should trust C or not. Guha et al. [2004] present and evaluate different possibilities of modeling distrust. According to their evaluation, using single step distrust propagation (if A distrusts B, B distrusts C, and C distrusts D, it is assumed that A will distrust C, but no assumption is made about the relationship between A and D) produces best results. In order to infer trust relationships in the normally poorly connected Web of Trust, a combination of all atomic trust propagation techniques forming the combined matrix $C_{B,\alpha}$ is used with $B = T$:

$$C_{B,\alpha} = \alpha_1 B + \alpha_2 B^T B, \alpha_3 B^T, \alpha_4 BB^T$$

where $\alpha = (\alpha_1, \alpha_2, \alpha_3, \alpha_4)$ is a vector representing weights for combining the four atomic propagation schemes, B is the belief matrix, and B^T is the transposed belief matrix. Entries in $C_{B,\alpha}$ indicate how trust can be propagated within the Web of Trust. To propagate the trust, it is necessary to apply $C_{B,\alpha}$ on the initial trust information available. Let $P^{(k)}$ be a propagation matrix where each entry describes how strong the trust is between users after k propagation steps: using a combination of $P^{(k)}$ with different propagation depths, a final propagation matrix F can be computed using a weighted linear combination:

$$F = \sum_{k=1}^{K} \gamma^k . P^{(k)}$$

where K is a suitably chosen integer and γ is a constant that is smaller than the largest eigenvalue of $C_{B,\alpha}$. K represents the maximal depth of trust propagation in the Web of Trust, γ is a parameter basically determining the rate of decay of trust as propagated within the Web of Trust (the further trust is propagated, the weaker it becomes). The most successful method presented by Guha and colleagues in Guha et al. [2004] is called *majority rounding*. The basic idea is to use information from the original belief matrix B to make assumptions about whether an inferred trust value should be interpreted as trust or distrust. Suppose a user i expresses trust and distrust for n people (entries in the trust matrix T or distrust matrix D), and we need to infer a trust relationship toward a user j. Using the final propagation matrix F, all inferred trust values linking i to the n users initially trusted or distrusted are sorted in the ascending order, including the entry f_{ij}. Then, depending on the local neighborhood of trust statements in the ordered set, f_{ij} is interpreted as trust or distrust, based on the majority of trust statements in the neighborhood.

4.4.2   AGGREGATION-BASED PROPAGATION

More generally, trust propagation algorithms work on DAGs extracted from potentially cyclic trust networks.

In order to perform propagation methods on that graph, certain properties of trust have to be assumed. Jennifer Golbeck [Golbeck, 2005] emphasized four properties as being central.

1. Transitivity. The basic idea of transitivity in trust models is that if A trusts B and B trusts C, then A should also trust C to some extent. The question on how trust should decay when being propagated is a modeling parameter and can vary depending on application needs.

2. Composability. The general idea of composability of trust is that if people get the same recommendation from different trusted sources, the trust assigned to that recommendation will be higher than if only one source is available.

3. Personalization. When dealing with humans interacting in trust networks, instead of computer agents, everybody will have his own idea of what trust is and whom to trust. The very same person will be trusted by some and mistrusted by others.

4. Asymmetry. The concept of asymmetry of trust is of importance when modeling trust in very anonymous settings like the Web. While A might find B's reviews helpful, B might not even know A. Therefore it makes no sense to assume all trust relationships would have to be mutual.

In aggregation-based approaches, trust value for a source in a target is predicted by aggregating the trust scores in the target from target's "trusted" neighbors weighted with trust value in the corresponding neighbor.

An approach called FACiLE (Faith Assessment Combining Last Edges) has been proposed which significantly improves the accuracy of trust inference avoiding the distortion caused by malicious behavior or subjectivity of one node above. The underlying idea is as follows: in order to make a trust assessment over a source of knowledge, simply ask its neighbors and adopt their assessment in a way that is based on their own relative inferred trust values. The approach is motivated from social networks, where every person knows her neighbors (i.e., persons with whom she socializes more frequently) better than anyone else. Given a trust graph G, the generalized Bellman-Ford algorithm given in Table 4.3 is used with $E^*(G)$, the set of edges that satisfy a threshold condition from each node and $t[v]$ the inferred trust for node v. Bellman-Ford's algorithm's original purpose is to measure shortest paths, and Chapter 5 will further introduce and develop its application to the modeling of complex networks.

Table 4.3: Generalized Bellman-Ford algorithm

$$
\begin{array}{l}
\text{for } i = 1 \text{ to } |V(G)| - 1 \\
\quad \text{for each edge } (u,v) \in E^*(G) \\
\quad\quad t[v] \leftarrow \oplus[t[v], t[u] \otimes t_{u,v}]
\end{array}
$$

with $\oplus$: aggregation and $\otimes$: concatenation

Example 4.4   The graph in Figure 4.3 depicts a trust graph which is built up to infer the trust of a source on the Semantic Web from Bintzios et al. [2006]. It is a directed graph with the trust assessment (values from 0 to 1) on each communication link between each two nodes (entities on the Web). There is a certain threshold of trust that has to be met in order for node q to trust anyone over the Web. In the example illustrated in Figure 4.3, we assume the threshold is 0.3. Consequently, entity b is not trusted because its trust assessment (0.2) by q is less than the threshold. Furthermore, q is trying to assess the trustworthiness of s by looking at the neighbors of s, which are b and d. The generalized Bellman-Ford Algorithm is used to find the inferred trust of a source's neighbor on the Web. Multiplication is used as concatenation operation and maximum for aggregation. Since $t_{q,b} = 0.2$, b mostly provides untrustworthy referrals. On the other hand, d appears to be considerably more trustworthy. The inferred trust for s will be $t_{q,s} = t_{d,s} = 0.6$ since q will take the direct trust value of the most trustworthy neighbor of s. We would have multiplied all the trust values of all the edges making one path to a neighbor of s and then taking the direct trust value of the neighbor with the highest inferred trust. If this value exceeds the threshold of trust then we will trust this node and trust it trust assessment of s. Moreover, if both b and d were untrustworthy, then their trust values as inferred by FACiLE would be very low (i.e., below trust threshold). Thus, s would be considered distrusted and could not be maliciously promoted by b and d.

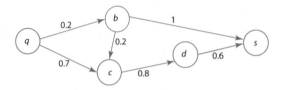

Figure 4.3: Example of trust graph.

4.5   CONCLUSION

In this chapter, we have presented a brief overview of the literature related to trust modeling, trust computation, and inference. We have focused on direct and indirect trust metrics and their mathematical representation with Beta and Dirichlet probability density distributions for direct trust computation, and we have presented some prevalent trust models that define trust propagation axioms or aggregation rules in various contexts. This chapter does intend to exhaustively cover trust research, whose goal is to develop expressive trust frameworks that have declarative, axiomatic, and computational specifications, and to devise methodologies for instantiating them for practical use of automatic trust/trustworthiness inference in terms of application-oriented semantics of trust. However, this incursion into trust analysis is relevant for truth discovery and data veracity estimation and hybrid methods combining iterative data/source voting algorithms as presented in Chapter 3, and source trust modeling and inference based on past direct and indirect experience could substantially improve the state-of-the art. A trust graph can also be interpreted as a layer of a source network which makes a perfect transition. The next chapter is devoted to complex network systems and the dynamics of rumors and misinformation.

CHAPTER 5

Misinformation Dynamics

5.1   INTRODUCTION

In March 2015, Facebook had over 1.44 billion monthly active users, according to the company's official figures. Around 65% of them were active on a daily basis.[1] Twitter claims to have more than 300 million users producing 500 million tweets each day.[2] By the end of 2014, mobile cellular subscriptions had scaled up to 96 per 100 inhabitants around the globe, of which more than 30% had broadband access, according to the International Telecommunication Union.[3] All these figures, with supralinear growth over the last decade, are indicative of the radical transformation that affects how we interact and communicate; they are also indicative that we confront an information explosion that is a threat—if we can't make sense of it—but above all a challenge and an opportunity. Indeed, the population's ever-growing digital footprint promises revolutionary advances in scientific disciplines, and also deep societal impacts—with effects ranging from leisure time, to economy and finance, to health and policy issues. Often referred to as Big Data (where "big" refers to storage size but also, and more specifically, to the higher spatial and temporal resolution of the data), the new sources of information require efficient approaches to data manipulation and exploitation, but also theoretical tools to model and scrutinize their inherent complexity—that is, the complexity of the social dynamics that the data track with unprecedented fidelity.

   Of all the lessons learned in the past years, the most compelling one might be the fact that Big Data challenges can seldom be attacked from a single specialized discipline: we are increasingly becoming aware that solutions may arrive from heterogeneous approaches, that combine apparently distant disciplines. This is how Computer Science (and in particular research on Data Quality and Truth Discovery), on one hand, and Statistical Physics (Complex Systems), on the other, may have to meet to tackle the problem of misinformation and data truthworthiness. To see how (or if) this can be done, we present in this chapter a number of theoretical and empirical findings which may pave the way toward a fruitful combination—the algorithmic power, storage capacity, and processing facilities from Computer Science, with the Science of Networks which, powered by digital data, has contributed to advance to new exciting grounds.

---

[1] http://newsroom.fb.com/company-info/, accessed June 2015.
[2] https://about.twitter.com/company, accessed June 2015.
[3] 2005-2015 ICT data for the world: http://www.itu.int/en/ITU-D/Statistics/Pages/facts/default.aspx. Released in May 2015, accessed in June 2015.

In this chapter, we will bring forward the main contributions that build up the understanding of how information propagates in networked systems, and associated problems. Figure 5.1 illustrates the chapter's outline.

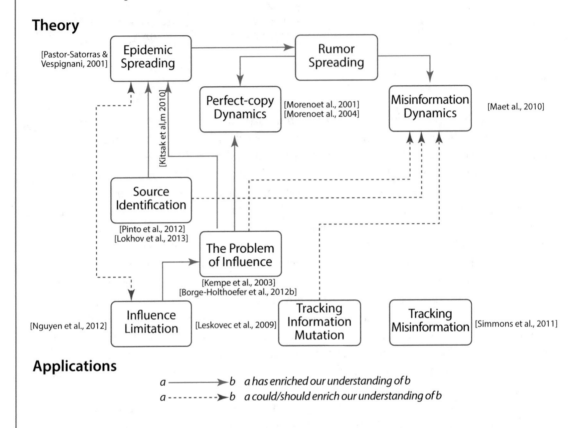

Figure 5.1: Chapter 5 roadmap. From top to bottom, every aspect surveyed in this chapter is represented. On the uppermost side we can see the purely theoretical contributions in the field of information diffusion, from a complex network perspective. This also includes the off-topic *epidemic spreading*, the theoretical precursor of rumor spreading. Topics between the Theory and Application poles have, to some degree, strong theoretical aspects but deal with/have been applied to real-world problems. Finally, some purely empirical contributions are included, for which practical solutions have been offered without a modeling or theoretical insight effort to them. Each block in this outline has incoming or outgoing connections, which represent inter-topic relationships (existing or potential, see legend). For each block, one or two representative citations have been included (although these are not exhaustive).

After some background on Complex Networks (Section 5.1), we will start presenting the theoretical foundations and various approaches for modeling diffusion phenomena, from disease propagation (stemming from Applied Mathematics and Epidemiology) to information spreading in networked systems (Section 5.2). Because social dynamics are inherently noisy (error-prone), in Section 5.3, we will revisit theoretical works on misinformation spreading as well—or how the mutation of a piece of information affects the system's capacity to deal with it. In Section 5.4, we will switch from theoretical work toward empirical results—which, unfortunately, are not yet abundant. The chapter will close with some conclusions.

5.2   THEORETICAL FOUNDATIONS

In the past 15 years we have witnessed the evolution of the field of Complex Networks. Of course, the novelty laid not in the well-known mathematical apparatus around graphs (which can be traced back for centuries), but rather in the existence—and availability—of large datasets, affordable computational power and the extensive statistical Physics framework. The confluence of these factors (mathematical formalism, viable technology, robust Physics-theoretical background) resulted in the unfolding of impactful applications, ranging from Social Sciences, Biology, Neuroscience, or Linguistics.

To explore the insights in the field of (mis)information dissemination, we need first a summary of some concepts for a full understanding of the remaining sections in the chapter. There is an extensive literature with many excellent reviews and books about the structure and dynamics of complex networks [Barrat et al., 2008, Boccaletti et al., 2006, Caldarelli, 2007, Dorogovtsev et al., 2008, Newman et al., 2006]. Here we present an overview of only those minimal requirements of the theory that will be mentioned in the current work.

5.2.1   TERMINOLOGY IN COMPLEX NETWORKS

A network G is a graph with N nodes and L links. Every graph may be represented in a matrix notation, through the so-called adjacency matrix, A, which is an $N \times N$ matrix where the entries, $a_{ij} = w_{ij}$, indicate the existence of a link of strength w_{ij} from vertex i to j. Adjacency matrices representing undirected networks are symmetric, $a_{ij} = a_{ji}$, whereas unweighted networks are represented by binary matrices, $a_{ij} \in \{0, 1\}$. If the network is *directed* links are then named *arcs*, and account for the directionality of the connections. Two vertices i and j are *adjacent*, or neighbors, if they have an edge connecting them. Notice that, in a directed network, i being adjacent to j does not entail j being adjacent to i: the adjacency matrix is in this case asymmetric. Networks with multiple links (multigraphs) or multiple layers (multiplexes) are not considered here.

A *path* in a network is a sequence of vertices $i_1, i_2, \ldots, i_n$ such that from each of its vertices there is an edge to the next vertex in the sequence. The first vertex is called the *start* vertex and the last vertex is called the *end* vertex. The *length* of the path or *distance* between i_1 and i_n is then the number of edges of the path, which is $n - 1$ in unweighted networks. For weighted networks, the length is the addition of each weight in every edge. When i_1 and i_n are identical, their distance is 0. When i_1 and i_n are unreachable from each other, their distance is defined to be infinity (∞).

A *connected network* is an undirected network such that there exists a path between all pairs of vertices. If the network is directed, and there exists a path from each vertex to every other

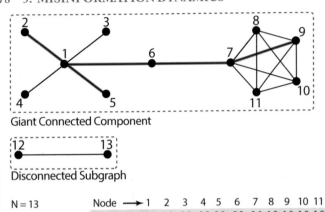

Giant Connected Component

Disconnected Subgraph

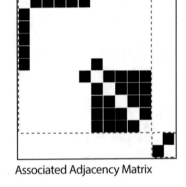

Associated Adjacency Matrix

$N = 13$
$L = 17$
$\langle k \rangle = 1.3$
$APL = 2.4$
$D = 4$

Node →	1	2	3	4	5	6	7	8	9	10	11	12	13
Clustering	0.0	0.0	0.0	0.0	0.0	0.0	0.6	1.0	1.0	1.0	1.0	0.0	0.0
Dc	0.4	0.0	0.0	0.0	0.0	0.1	0.4	0.3	0.3	0.3	0.3	0.0	0.0
Bc	0.4	0.0	0.0	0.0	0.0	0.3	0.3	0.0	0.0	0.0	0.0	0.0	0.0
Ec	0.0	0.0	0.0	0.0	0.0	0.1	0.4	0.4	0.4	0.4	0.4	0.0	0.0
Core	1	1	1	1	1	1	2	2	2	2	2	1	1

Figure 5.2: Example graph with $N = 13$ nodes and $L = 17$ edges. The undirected, unweighted graph is a disconnected one (we can observe a giant component, nodes 1 to 11; and a disconnected subgraph, nodes 12 and 13). This of course is reflected in the corresponding adjacency matrix (right), where the different components are outlined in red. Interestingly, nodes 1 to 5 conform a very sparse subgraph (star-shaped), whereas nodes 7 to 11 build a *complete* subgraph. Some of the main global descriptors are included, such as average degree ($\langle k \rangle$), average path length (APL), or Diameter (D). Some *micro* (i.e., node-level) descriptors are outlined, such as per-node clustering coefficient and some centrality measures (C_D, C_B and C_A). Note that centrality measures are not necessarily correlated: node 6 has a small centrality degree-wise, but such description is at odds with the C_B, for instance. (Note: all values have been truncated to a single decimal position).

vertex, then it is a *strongly connected network*. A network is considered to be a *complete network* if all vertices are connected to one another by one edge. We denote the complete network on n vertices K_n. A *clique* in a network is a set of pairwise adjacent vertices. Since any subnetwork induced by a clique is a complete subnetwork, the two terms and their notations are usually used interchangeably. A k-clique is a clique of order k. A *maximal clique* is a clique that is not a subset of any other clique.

See Figure 5.2 for an illustrative example of the main concepts in the description of the structure of a network.

5.2.2   COMPLEX NETWORK DESCRIPTORS

Degree and Degree Distribution

The simplest and the most intensively studied one vertex characteristic is degree. Degree, k, of a vertex is the total number of its connections. If we are dealing with a directed graph, in-degree, k_{in}, is the number of incoming arcs of a vertex. Out-degree, k_{out} is the number of its outgoing arcs. Degree is actually the number of nearest neighbors of a vertex. The total distributions of vertex degrees of an entire network, $p(k)$, with $p(k_{in})$ the in-degree distribution, and $p(k_{out})$ the out-degree distribution, are its basic statistical characteristics. We define $p(k)$ to be the fraction of vertices in the network that have degree k. Equivalently, $p(k)$ is the probability that a vertex chosen uniformly at random has degree k. Most of the work in network theory deals with cumulative degree distributions, noted $P(k)$. A plot of $P(k)$ for any given network is built through a cumulative histogram of the degrees of vertices. Although the degree of a vertex is a local quantity, the cumulative degree distribution often determines some important global characteristics of networks. We want to highlight at this point an important one: Given a network G, the particular probability distribution that fits its $P(k)$ is a *signature* of the class of networks G belongs to. Random graphs [Erdös and Rényi, 1959] and small-world networks (Watts–Strogatz model [Watts and Strogatz, 1998]) display $P(k)$ distributions that follow a Poisson distribution. Whereas scale-free networks [Barabási and Albert, 1999] produce a degree distribution $P(k) \approx k^{-\gamma}$. Several empirical results show evidence that many large networks are scale-free, that is, their degree distribution follows a power law for large k with the existence of a few hyper-connected nodes—the *hubs*. From $P(k)$ we can calculate the moments of the distribution. The n-moment of $P(k)$ is defined as

$$\langle k^n \rangle = \sum_{k}^{N} k^n p(k) \tag{5.1}$$

The first moment $\langle k \rangle$ is the mean degree of the network.

Shortest Path and Diameter

For each pair of vertices i and j connected by at least one path, one can introduce the shortest path length, the so-called *intervertex distance* d_{ij}, the corresponding number of edges in the shortest path. Then one can define the distribution of the shortest-path lengths between pairs of vertices of a network and the average shortest path length APL of a network. The average here is over all pairs of vertices between which a path exists. It determines the effective "linear size" of a network, i.e., the average separation of pairs of vertices. In a fully connected network, $d = 1$. Recall that shortest paths can also be measured in weighted networks, then the path's cost equals the sum of the weights. One can also introduce the maximal intervertex distance over all the pairs of vertices between which a path exists. This descriptor determines the maximal extent of a network; the maximal shortest path is also referred to as the *diameter* (D) of the network.

Clustering Coefficient

The presence of connections between the nearest neighbors of a vertex i is described by its clustering coefficient. Suppose that a node (or vertex) i in the network has k_i edges and they connect this node to k_i other nodes. These nodes are all neighbors of node i. Clearly, at most

$$\binom{k_i}{2} = \frac{k_i(k_i - 1)}{2} \qquad (5.2)$$

edges can exist among them, and this occurs when every neighbor of node i is connected to every other neighbor of node i. This represents the number of loops of length 3 attached to vertex i. The clustering coefficient C_i of node i is then defined as the ratio between the number E_i of edges that actually exist among these k_i nodes and the total possible number:

$$C_i = \frac{2E_i}{k_i(k_i - 1)} \qquad (5.3)$$

Equivalently, the clustering coefficient of a node i can be defined as the proportion of 3-cliques in which i participates. The clustering coefficient C of the whole network is the average of C_i over all i. Clearly, $C \leq 1$; and $C = 1$ if and only if the network is globally coupled, which means that every node in the network connects to every other node. By definition, *trees* are graphs without loops, i.e., $C = 0$.

   The clustering coefficient of the network reflects the transitivity of the mean closest neighborhood of a network vertex, that is, the extent to which the nearest neighbors of a vertex are the nearest neighbors of each other [Watts and Strogatz, 1998]. The notion of clustering was introduced much earlier in Sociology [Wasserman and Faust, 1994].

Centrality Measures

Centrality measures are some of the most fundamental and frequently used measures of network structure. Centrality measures address the question: "Which is the most important or central node in this network?," that is, the question whether nodes should all be considered equal in significance or not (whether some kind of hierarchy exists in the system). The existence of such hierarchy would then imply that certain vertices in the network are more *central* than others. There are many answers to this question, depending on what we mean by "important." Here we briefly explore three centrality indexes (betweenness, k-core, and eigenvector centrality) that are widely used in the network literature. Note however that these are not the only method to classify nodes' importance. Within graph theory and network analysis, there are various measures of the centrality of a vertex. For instance, there are two other main centrality measures that are widely used in network analysis: *degree centrality* C_D and *closeness*. C_D, the simplest, assumes that the larger the degree of a node, the more central it is. The closeness centrality of a vertex measures how easily other vertices can be reached from it (or the other way: how easily it can be reached from the other vertices). It is defined as the number of vertices minus one divided by the sum of the lengths of all geodesics from/to the given vertex.

Betweenness   One of the first significant attempts to solve the question of node centrality is Freeman's proposal (originally posed from a Social Science point of view): *betweenness* as a centrality measure [Freeman, 1977]. As Freeman points out, a node in a network is central to the extent that it falls on the shortest path between pairs of other nodes. In his own words, "suppose that in order for node i to contact node j, node k must be used as an intermediate station. Node k in such a context has a certain 'responsibility' to nodes i and j. If we count all the minimum paths that pass through node k, then we have a measure of the 'stress' which node k must undergo during the activity of the network. A vector giving this number for each node of the network would give us a good idea of stress conditions throughout the system" [Freeman, 1977]. Computationally, betweenness is measured according to the next equation:

$$C_B(i) = \sum_{j \neq i \neq k} \frac{\sigma_{jk}(i)}{\sigma_{jk}} \tag{5.4}$$

with σ_{jk} as the number of shortest paths from j to k, and $\sigma_{jk}(i)$ the number of shortest paths from j to k that pass through vertex i. Note that shortest paths can be measured in a weighted and/or directed network, thus it is possible to calculate this descriptor for any network [Brandes, 2001]. Commonly, betweenness is normalized by dividing through by the number of pairs of vertices not including the considered node i, which is $(n-1)(n-2)$. By means of normalization, it is possible to compare the betweenness of nodes from different networks.

k-core   The k-core offers another local property that relies on global network structure. This metric gauges the existence of cohesive subgroups of nodes in a network. The network can be seen as a set of successively enclosed substructures or k-cores, comprising vertices having at least degree k. This partition of the whole graph assigns an integer number to every node in the network obtained by a recursive pruning of the vertices. One starts with isolated nodes, which are assigned a $k_c = 0$. Then vertices with $k = 1$ are removed along with their links, and assigned $k_c = 1$. If any of the remaining nodes is left with k connections it is also removed and contained in the $k_c = 1$ core. The process continues with $k_c = 2, 3, \ldots$ until every node has been assigned to a k_c shell. This measure of centrality goes beyond degree because it takes into account the centrality of a vertex's neighbors to define the centrality of that vertex.

Eigenvector centrality   A more sophisticated version of the degree centrality is the so-called eigenvector centrality C_A [Bonacich, 1972]. Where degree centrality gives a simple count of the number of connections a vertex has, eigenvector centrality acknowledges that not all connections are equal. In general, connections to people who are themselves influential will lend a person more influence than connections to less influential people. If we denote the centrality of vertex i by x_i, then we can allow for this effect by making x_i proportional to the average of the centralities of i's network neighbors:

$$x_i = \frac{1}{\lambda} \sum_{j=1}^{N} A_{ij} x_j \qquad (5.5)$$

where λ is a constant. Defining the vector of centralities $x = (x_1, x_2, \dots)$, we can rewrite this equation in matrix form as

$$\lambda x = Ax \qquad (5.6)$$

and hence we see that x is an eigenvector of the adjacency matrix with eigenvalue λ. Assuming that we wish the centralities to be non-negative, it can be shown (using the Perron-Frobenius theorem [Berman and Plemmons, 1979]) that λ must be the largest eigenvalue of the adjacency matrix and x the corresponding eigenvector.

The eigenvector centrality defined in this way assigns each vertex a centrality that depends both on the number and the quality of its connections: having a large number of connections still counts for something, but a vertex with a smaller number of high-quality contacts may outrank one with a larger number of mediocre contacts. In other words, eigenvector centrality assigns relative scores to all nodes in the network based on the principle that connections to high-scoring nodes contribute more to the score of the node in question than equal connections to low-scoring nodes.

Eigenvector centrality turns out to be a revealing measure in many situations. For example, a variant of eigenvector centrality is employed by the well-known Web search engine Google to rank webpages, and works well in that context. Specifically, from an abstract point of view, the World Wide Web forms a directed graph, in which nodes are webpages and the edges between them are hyperlinks [Adamic, 1999]. The goal of a search engine is to retrieve an ordered list of pages that are relevant to a particular query. Typically, this is done by identifying all pages that contain the words that appear in the query, then ordering those pages using a measure of their importance based on their link structure. Although the details of the algorithms used by commercial search engines are proprietary, the basic principles behind the PageRank algorithm (part of Google search engine) are public knowledge [Page et al., 1998], and such algorithm relies on the concept of eigenvector centrality.

5.2.3   NETWORK MODELS

Regular Graphs

Although regular graphs do not fall under the definition of complex networks (they are actually quite far from being complex, thus their name), they play an important role in the understanding of the concept of "small world." For this reason we offer a brief comment on them.

In graph theory, a regular graph is a graph where each vertex has the same number of neighbors, i.e., every vertex has the same degree. A regular graph with vertices of degree k is called a k-regular graph or regular graph of degree k [Read and Wilson, 1998].

Random Graphs

Before the burst of attention on complex networks in the 1990s, a particularly rich source of ideas has been the study of random graphs, graphs in which the edges are distributed randomly. Networks with a complex topology and unknown organizing principles often appear random; thus random-graph theory is regularly used in the study of complex networks. The theory of random graphs was introduced by Paul Erdös and Alfréd Rényi [Erdös and Rényi, 1959] after Erdös discovered that probabilistic methods were often useful in tackling problems in graph theory. A detailed review of the field is available in the classic book of Bollobás [Bollobás, 2001]. Here we briefly describe the most important results of random graph theory, focusing on the aspects that are of direct relevance to complex networks.

In their classic first article on random graphs, Erdös and Rényi define a random graph as N labeled nodes connected by L edges, which are chosen randomly from the $N(N-1)/2$ possible edges [Erdös and Rényi, 1959].

In a random graph with connection probability p, the degree k_i of a node i follows a binomial distribution with parameters $N-1$ and p:

$$P(k_i = k) = \binom{N-1}{k} p^k (1-p)^{N-1-k} \tag{5.7}$$

The distribution of the N_k values, $P(N_k = r)$, approaches a Poisson distribution,

$$P(N_k = r) = \frac{\lambda_k^r}{r!} e^{-\lambda_k} \tag{5.8}$$

Thus the number of nodes with degree k follows a Poisson distribution with mean value λ_k.

Although random graph theory is elegant and simple, real-world phenomena interpreted and projected to a network by current science is not ruled by randomness. The established links between the nodes of various domains of reality follow fundamental natural laws. Despite the fact that some edges might be randomly set up, and they might play a non-negligible role, randomness is not the main feature in real networks. Therefore, the development of new models to capture real-life systems' features other than randomness has motivated novel approaches. In particular, two of these new models occupy a prominent place in contemporary thinking about complex networks. Here we define and briefly discuss them.

Watts–Strogatz Small-world Network

In simple terms, the small-world concept describes the fact that despite their often large size, in most networks there is a relatively short path between any two nodes. The distance between two nodes is defined as the number of edges along the shortest path connecting them. The most popular manifestation of small worlds is the "six degrees of separation" concept, uncovered by the social psychologist Stanley Milgram [Milgram, 1967, Travers and Milgram, 1969], who concluded that there was a path of acquaintances with a typical length of about six between most pairs of people in the United States.

This feature (short path lengths) is also present in random graphs. However, in a random graph, since the edges are distributed randomly, the clustering coefficient is considerably small. Instead, in most (if not all) real-world networks, the clustering coefficient is typically much larger than the one in a comparable random network (i.e., same number of nodes and edges as the real-world network).

Beyond Milgram's experiment, it was not until 1998 that Watts and Strogatz's work [Watts and Strogatz, 1998] stimulated the study of such phenomena. Their main discovery was the distinctive combination of high clustering with short characteristic path length, which is typical in real-world networks (either social, biological, or technological) that cannot be captured by traditional approximations such as those based on regular lattices or random graphs. From a computational point of view, Watts and Strogatz proposed a one-parameter model that interpolates between an ordered finite dimensional lattice and a random graph. The algorithm behind the model is the following [Watts and Strogatz, 1998]:

- *Start with order*: Start with a ring lattice with N nodes in which every node is connected to its first k neighbors ($k/2$ on either side). In order to have a sparse but connected network at all times, consider $N \gg k \gg ln(N) \gg 1$.

- *Randomize*: Randomly rewire each edge of the lattice with probability p_{rew} such that self-connections and duplicate edges are excluded. This process introduces $pNK/2$ long-range edges which connect nodes that otherwise would be part of different neighborhoods. By varying p_{rew} one can closely monitor the transition between order ($p_{rew} = 0$) and randomness ($p_{rew} = 1$).

The simple but interesting result when applying the algorithm was the following. Even for a small probability of rewiring, when the local properties of the network are still nearly the same as for the original regular lattice and the average clustering coefficient does not differ essentially from its initial value, the average shortest-path length is already of the order of the one for classical random graphs (see Figure 5.3).

As discussed in Watts and Strogatz [1998], the origin of the rapid drop in the average path length APL is the appearance of shortcuts between nodes. Every shortcut, created at random, is likely to connect widely separated parts of the graph, and thus has a significant impact on the characteristic path length of the entire graph. Even a relatively low fraction of shortcuts is sufficient to drastically decrease the average path length, yet locally the network remains highly ordered. In addition to a short average path length, small-world networks have a relatively high clustering coefficient. The Watts–Strogatz small-world model (SW) displays this duality for a wide range of the rewiring probabilities p_{rew}. In a regular lattice the clustering coefficient does not depend on the size of the lattice but only on its topology. As the edges of the network are randomized, the clustering coefficient remains close to the original one up to relatively large values of p_{rew}.

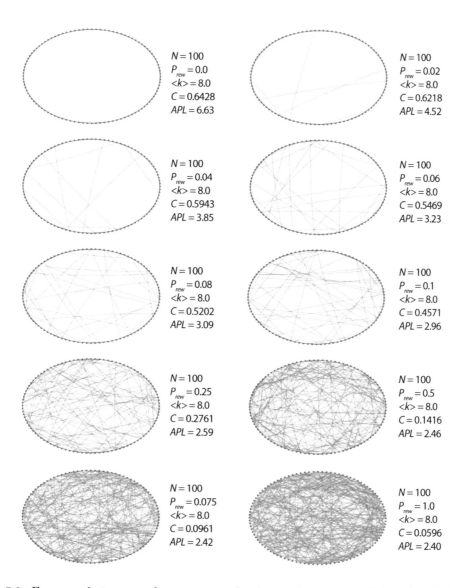

Figure 5.3: From regularity to randomness: note the changes in average path length and clustering coefficient as a function of the rewiring probability for the family of randomly rewired graphs. For low rewiring probabilities the clustering is still close to its initial value, whereas the average path length rapidly decreases. For the highest probability, the clustering has dropped to an order of 10^{-2}. This figure illustrates the fact that small-world is not *a* network, but a family of networks.

Scale-free Networks

Certainly, the SW model initiated a revival of network modeling in the past few years. However, there are some real-world phenomena that small-world networks can't capture, the most relevant one being evolution. In 1999, Barabási and Albert presented some data and formal work that has led to the construction of various scale-free models that, by focusing on the network dynamics, aim to offer a universal theory of network evolution [Barabási and Albert, 1999].

Several empirical results demonstrate that many large networks are scale-free (SF), that is, their degree distribution follows a power law for large k. The important question is then: what is the mechanism responsible for the emergence of scale-free networks? Answering this question requires a shift from modeling network topology to modeling the network assembly and evolution. While the goal of the former models is to construct a graph with correct topological features, the modeling of scale-free networks will put the emphasis on capturing the network dynamics.

In the first place, the network models discussed up to now (random and small-world) assume that graphs start with a fixed number N of vertices that are then randomly connected or rewired, without modifying N. In contrast, most real-world networks describe open systems that *grow* by the continuous addition of new nodes. Starting from a small nucleus of nodes, the number of nodes increases throughout the lifetime of the network by the subsequent addition of new nodes. For example, the World Wide Web grows exponentially in time by the addition of new webpages.

Second, network models discussed so far assume that the probability that two nodes are connected (or their connection is rewired) is independent of the nodes degree, i.e., new edges are placed randomly. Most real-world networks, however, exhibit *preferential attachment,* such that the likelihood of connecting to a node depends on the nodes' degree. For example, a webpage will more likely include hyperlinks to popular documents with already high degrees, because such highly connected documents are easy to find and thus well-known.

These two ingredients, growth and preferential attachment, inspired the introduction of the Barabási–Albert model (BA), which led for the first time to a network with a power-law degree distribution. The algorithm of the BA model is the following:

1. *Growth*: Starting with a small number (m_0) of nodes, at every time step, we add a new node with m edges ($m \leq m_0$) that link the new node to m different nodes already present in the system;

2. *Preferential attachment*: When choosing the nodes to which the new node connects, we assume that the probability Π_i that a new node will be connected to node i depends on the degree k_i, such that

$$\Pi_i = \frac{k_i}{\sum_j k_j} \qquad (5.9)$$

It is specially in step (1) of the algorithm that the scale-free model captures the dynamics of a system. The power-law scaling in the BA model indicates that growth and preferential attachment play important roles in network development. However, some questions arise when considering step (2): Admitting that new nodes' attachment might be preferential, is there only one equation (specifically, the one mentioned here) that grasps such preference across different networks (e.g., social, technological, etc.)? Can preferential attachment be expressed otherwise?

In the limit $t \to \infty$ (network with infinite size), the BA model produces a degree distribution $P(k) \approx k^{-\gamma}$ with an exponent $\gamma = 3$. This setting is often used to produce synthetic networks, on which different dynamics can be tested as we shall see in the remainder of the chapter (we will refer to these topologies as SF networks).

5.3   DISEASE AND RUMOR PROPAGATION MODELS

Models on information diffusion (rumor spreading) appeared initially as derivations from epidemiological literature, because of the similarity of the "contagion" dynamics: an agent (in the "inactive," "susceptible," or "ignorant" state) that decides whether to adopt a given state as a function of the neighboring agents who have already adopted it (i.e., "active" agents or in the "infectious" or "spreader" class). In both epidemic- and rumor-like dynamics, the decisions to adopt are taken independently with probability p for each successive contact.

These models, despite their theoretical character, have been key to build up an analytical framework, i.e., a minimum set of concepts that allow for an idealized understanding of the driving mechanisms of such processes. In the absence of appropriate data, simulation and analytical models were developed under the influence of two streams of research: epidemiological studies [Bailey and Bailey, 1975, Hethcote, 2000, Murray, 1993] and rumor dynamics [Daley and Kendall, 1964, Goffman and Newill, 1964, Rapoport, 1953], and can be traced back as much as five decades.

5.3.1   EPIDEMIC SPREADING

The mathematics of epidemic spreading were originally developed, unsurprisingly, in the fields of Medicine and Biology [Bailey and Bailey, 1975]. Their application to information propagation has been rather indirect, through physicists and computer scientists who found in epidemic spreading a fecund metaphor of information propagation. This approach assumes that information travels through social networks as viral infections and that personal interactions open the diffusion routes [Daley and Kendall, 1964, Goffman and Newill, 1964]. According to these models, contagion dynamics evolve following a simple scheme: at each time step, infected individuals propagate the contagion to susceptible neighbors with probability λ. Additionally, infected individuals can recover at a rate μ (as in the susceptible-infected-recovered or SIR models); or they can revert to the susceptible state with probability μ (as in the susceptible-infected-susceptible or SIS models) [Hethcote, 2000]. These transitions can be expressed as differential equations under a simple form, which yield valuable insights within the framework of complex networks.

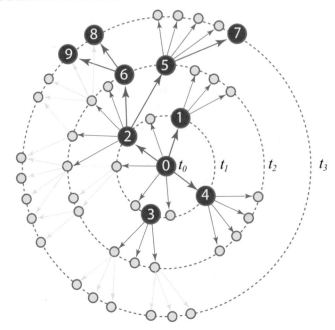

Figure 5.4: The notion of cascade. Nodes are disposed in concentric circles indicating the time when they received a specific tweet. Links between them represent the follower/friend relationship: an arrow from i to j indicates that j receives the disease/information from i. Red nodes are those who participate in the cascading process, whereas gray nodes remain unaffected ("susceptible" in disease spreading; "ignorant" in rumor dynamics). In this particular example, node 0 acts as the initial seed, emitting a message at time t_0 to its nearest neighbors. Some of them (nodes 1, 2, 3, and 4) join the cascade at the following time step t_1. The process continues and the cascade grows in size as new nodes become "infected." The process ends when no additional nodes are added to the process. Adapted from Baños et al. [2013].

Part of the interest in these dynamics is to learn what is the expected final size of affected nodes, also termed *cascade size*. The concept of "cascade" slightly varies across different types of dynamics (specially regarding the conditions to consider that the dynamics have reached an equilibrium, t i.e., no more nodes are added to the process). See Figure 5.4 for an illustration. Depending on the parameters of the dynamics, the final size of a cascade might be negligible (if the parameters lay below a certain *critical point*) or it can go global (above the critical point) [Gómez et al., 2010]. For instance, Pastor-Satorras and Vespignani [Pastor-Satorras and Vespignani, 2001] analytically established, for the SIS model, that the critical point (or *epidemic threshold*) in uncorrelated scale-free networks is given by $\lambda_c = \langle k \rangle / \langle k^2 \rangle$, leading to $\lambda_c \to 0$ as $N \to \infty$ when $2 < \gamma \le 3$. In practice, this means that for SF networks with a large size, the critical point is close to 0, i.e., any spreading process goes global.

Taking this as a starting point, Leskovec et al. exploit epidemic processes to replicate real information cascade size distributions in the blogosphere [Leskovec et al., 2007]. We already learn from these basic setups that an epidemic dynamics (and also information dynamics) output is of course dependent on the internal parameters (λ, μ) of the process, but it is *also* heavily constrained by structure ("on what kind of substrate is the dynamical process happening?"). And more particularly, the class of scale-free networks is extremely efficient at spreading infections (or information, for that matter). As a practical example of epidemic dynamics on real-world scenarios, Leskovec et al. [Leskovec et al., 2007] reproduce the most frequent information cascades, taking the blog network (i.e., blogs which contain pointers to other blogs) and tuning the infection probability on a SIS model.

5.3.2   RUMOR PROPAGATION

Rumor diffusion models sprung directly from the canonical SIR, renaming the susceptible, infected, and recovered classes to ignorant ("I," who has not heard the rumor yet), spreader ("S," who knows the rumor and is "infecting" ignorants), and stifler ("R," who also knows the rumor, but has decided not to spread it further). In this respect, again the chances of a rumor becoming global depend on the underlying structure and the particular parameters of the simulation.

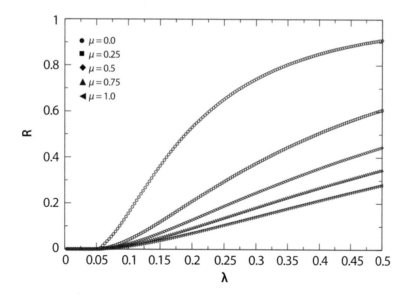

Figure 5.5: The final size of the rumor, R is shown as a function of the spreading rate λ for an SF network with size $N = 10^6$. The results are shown for several values of the stifling parameter μ. Note that higher stifling probabilities (μ) deliver smaller rumor outreach. Adapted from Nekovee et al. [2007].

Although rumor models are often regarded as a simple mapping of its epidemic counterpart, a number of differences set them apart. First, SIR is an attempt to model a real-world process, whereas researchers on rumor dynamics—which typically seek to maximize influence for the sake of technological and commercial applications—are free to design the rules of epidemic infection in order to reach the desired result. This affects mainly the transition from spreader to stifler [Nekovee et al., 2007], which can be implemented under different plausible forms. Second, rumor models can be applied to social systems the connectivity of which can be changed: For instance, in peer-to-peer file sharing systems, the connectivity distribution of the nodes can be changed in order to maximize the performance of the protocols, as informed by the models [Moreno et al., 2004]. Third, the dynamics are also different: the transition to the class of "recovered" in SIR happens spontaneously (at a certain rate), while classical rumor spreading allows the transition to "stifle" (at a certain rate) only after a "spreader" interacts with either another spreader or a stifler, i.e., spreaders learn that the rumor has lost its "news value" when they encounter neighbors already informed. For all these reasons, the outcomes of the rumor model may present significant differences when compared to simulations of SIR models. Mathematically, the general model can be represented as:

$$I \xrightarrow{\lambda} S$$
$$S \xrightarrow{\mu} R$$

where λ and μ represent the rumor adoption and cease probabilities, respectively. In typical simulations, initial conditions are set such that $i(0) = 1 - 1/N$, $\rho(0) = 1/N$ and $r(0) = 0$, i.e., the whole population is ignorant, except for a single initial spreader that triggers the rumor. These conditions are randomly set in each iteration, and final results are obtained via averaging of a large number of executions. For instance, Figure 5.5 depicts the rumor coverage (R, the fraction of nodes that learned about the initial rumor at the steady state) as a function of the spreading rate λ, where results are averaged over 300 runs with different initial random spreaders. Noteworthy, the rumor threshold (the point at which the rumor can reach a non-zero fraction of the population) is topology-dependent: for a given network, such a threshold does not change regardless of the stifling probability (μ). We learn then that some aspects of the dynamics are ruled by the particular structure of the network, whereas some others depend heavily on the parameters of the dynamics.

On the other hand, a *micro* approach may also be taken, by paying attention to how simulations change as a function of some feature of the initial condition. Figure 5.6 does this, so that it is possible to appreciate how a different initial spreader (with different levels of connectivity k) can affect the final outcome of the dynamics: as the connectivity of the seed is increased, the time it takes for the rumor to reach the asymptotic value decreases, so that for a fixed time length the number of individuals in the stifler class is higher when k_i gets larger.

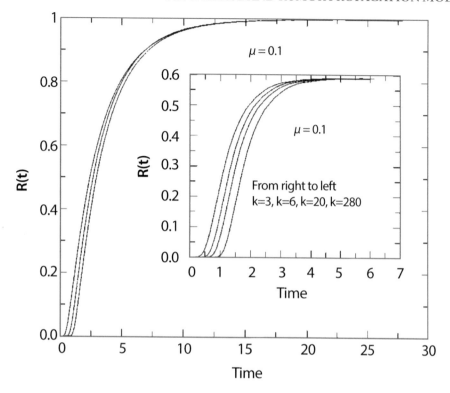

Figure 5.6: Density of stiflers as a function of time for $\mu = 0.1$ (main figure) and $\mu = 1.0$ (inset) when the initial spreader has the connectivity k indicated in the inset ($k = 3$ and $k = 6$ indistinguishable in main figure). Note that in all cases the final density of individuals who have learned the rumor is the same, but the asymptotic value is reached at different times. This points to the fact that nodes with a larger k have different dynamic characteristics. Simulations are run on SF networks, the system size is $N = 10^4$, $\langle k \rangle = 6$ and $\gamma = 3$. Adapted from Moreno et al. [2004].

5.3.3   MISINFORMATION DYNAMICS

Admittedly, rumor propagation processes in actual scenarios hardly ever occur in the way we have described—an unchanged piece of information spreading on a structured population until some equilibrium is reached. In realistic situations, distortion of the transmitted entity during the spreading process should be expected: mutation in word-of-mouth processes ("telephone game"), errors in transported data packets, or simply purposefully modified information are very likely to happen. Distortion in communication is inevitable and contributes partially to the growth of information—already large in these times. Information quality and veracity becomes then an issue of increasing importance, with implications ranging from personal privacy to national security [Doyle et al., 2001], and practical questions regarding which is the "true" original message, or who is the original source of it.

In front of this situation, very few works have generalized classical rumor spreading to accommodate these (otherwise intuitive) phenomena. Interestingly, now the question is not only about *what fraction* of a population will be reached by a rumor, but actually *which* are the conditions for information overflows in the system (with the recurrent question: How do the network features and the parameters of the dynamics constraint the final output?). In the work of Ma et al. [Ma et al., 2010] the authors introduce a message mutation probability p, which determines how often a message traveling from node i to node j will undergo distortion. It is easy to see that for $p = 0$, we recover the classical approach; whereas for $p > 0$ not one, but several messages can coexist in the network. Here lies one of the interesting results in this work: for small values of p, a steady state arises where the average number of messages on the network settles to a constant. For large values of p, however, the number of distinct messages increases with time—it diverges, unless a "node memory" constraint is placed (i.e., the number of different messages a node can be simultaneously aware of). Such differentiated scenarios imply that a critical probability p_c exists, below which different versions of a message coexist, but its number does not grow in time—information explosion can be controlled. And a region above p_c leading to information explosion. Of course, p_c depends not only on the described dynamics, but also on the particular structure of the underlying network. For instance, the authors use a tuning parameter β that modifies only the weight of the links in the network. Even this slight structural manipulation heavily affects the point at which information explosion can occur. Indeed, the nodes' neighborhood remains constant, but the strength of the connections vary, see Figure 5.7). Analytical insights—how p_c depends on the various parameters of the model—can be checked from the original work of Ma et al.

On the other hand, the question arises as well to whether different network models (random, small-world, scale-free) behave differently, given the same set of parameters. The answer to that comes from Jacobi & Ben-Assuli [Jacobi and Ben-Assuli, 2011], who claim that scale-free networks are less sensitive to data distortion because of the existence of *hubs*. Hubs and high-degree nodes receive a message at an early stage of the propagation, and they deliver it to a large fraction of the network. Therefore, fewer message distortions occur in the propagation process. This is of course noteworthy because many real-world networks (and particularly online social networks, where much of the information is created and transmitted) fall under the scale-free type of network. Also, we already mentioned—and we will get back to it later—that hubs can shape significantly the behavior of a dynamical process.

5.4   THEORY UNDER TEST: EMPIRICAL FEEDBACK

Some of the theoretical developments from the previous section have received a fair amount of attention from researchers who attempt to seek empirical—beyond merely qualitative—validation. Unfortunately—as we shall see—these efforts have focused on the epidemic and rumor spread-

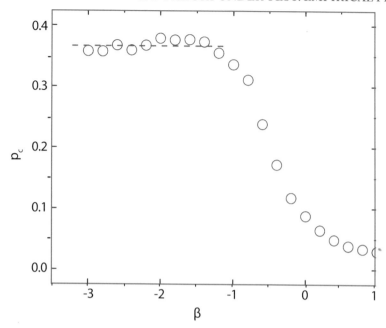

Figure 5.7: Critical distortion probability p_c as a function of the control parameter β. Simulations have been run on an ensemble of synthetic scale-free networks, with $N = 500$ nodes and average degree $\langle k \rangle = 6$. The data points are obtained by numerical simulations and the dash line is the analytical estimation. Adapted from Ma et al. [2010].

ing in their most idealized form, where no mutation or misinformation arises. And yet they pose interesting enough questions and results, which give room to some future research directions in the area.

5.4.1 SOURCE IDENTIFICATION

In many real-world situations, researchers don't have information about where a diffusive process has begun. If we think of the latest Ebola or MERS outbreaks during 2014, we immediately perceive the importance of accessing this information, to infer more accurate predictions on disease spreading and better decision-making to mitigate the effects. Likewise—in a less dramatic setting—the trustworthiness of a piece of information may be different if we discover the source of it. Back to the Ebola example, a tweet might be differently perceived—and spread—if its author is the World Health Organization (WHO) vs. an unreliable, anonymous individual. These considerations point to the problem of *data provenance* as stated in Chapter 1, in the framework of networked systems—and particularly, social networks.

Admittedly, finding the source of a tweet is an easy task, provided the digital trace that *an unmodified message* leaves behind. But, more often than not, that is not the case (see Section 5.5). Also, in order to make the estimation of the origin of spreading a well-defined problem we need to have some knowledge about the spreading mechanism [Lokhov et al., 2014]. Therefore, our capacity to design spreading-dynamics-aware, misinformation-aware algorithms is a new line of exploratory research.

Such research has, so far, been limited to epidemic scenarios [Agaskar and Lu, 2013, Lokhov et al., 2014, Pinto et al., 2012]. Pinto et al. [2012] turn away from the *forward problem* of epidemics (understanding the diffusion process), to focus on the *inverse problem*, by which they attempt to infer (providing, thus, estimations) the original source of diffusion. While previous work had focused on the inverse problem, this work is one of the first to do so with scalability in mind. Their proposal starts off with two constraints: (i) the networks underlying the dynamics are presumed to be large and sparse (which fits our empirical experience for most natural and man-made networks; and social networks particularly); (ii) we ignore the state of *every* node in the network, i.e., only a small fraction of nodes can be observed.

The logic behind Pinto et al.'s work is that, given a sufficiently rich set of observers, the source of the process can be estimated. And it can be done avoiding the intractability of a straightforward maximum likelihood approach, which demands integrating over *all possible paths* along which the infection (or information) has traveled to the observers, and over *all propagation delays*, i.e., the times at which the observer received the infection (or information).

Instead, and for the general case of an arbitrary graph G, they adopt a heuristics which assumes that diffusion takes place on a breadth-first-search (BFS) tree—a strong assumption by which infection travels from the source to each observer along a minimum-length path. Under this framework, they test the algorithm for different synthetic networks. The results are very illustrative, see Table 5.1.

Table 5.1: Fraction of observers needed to achieve a reliable (90%) estimation of the process source, for different small ($N = 100$) networks and observer placement (high degree, random)

Network	High degree	Random
scale-free, $\gamma = 3$	0.18	0.41
random	0.32	0.44

From Table 5.1 we learn that in a synthetic (i.e., simulated) scenario the algorithm requires a small fraction of nodes to deliver good estimations regarding the origin of the spreading process. Furthermore, the scheme is tested against a real-world case; see Figure 5.8.

Interestingly, when observers are chosen among the best connected, the fraction needed is dramatically smaller than in any other case. It is no surprise that hardly any improvement is gained in the random network case: homogeneous by construction, highly connected nodes are actually

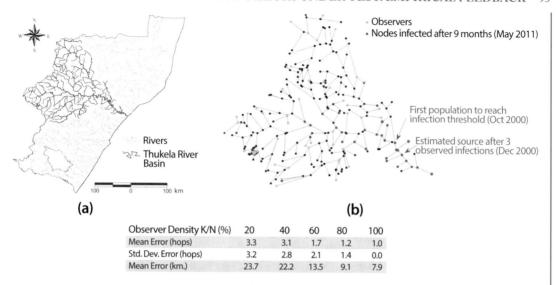

Observer Density K/N (%)	20	40	60	80	100
Mean Error (hops)	3.3	3.1	1.7	1.2	1.0
Std. Dev. Error (hops)	3.2	2.8	2.1	1.4	0.0
Mean Error (km.)	23.7	22.2	13.5	9.1	7.9

Figure 5.8: Locating the source of a cholera outbreak in South Africa. (a) Hydrographic map of the affected province. The red dot indicates the location of the first reported cases of cholera. (b) Graphical model of the Thukela river basin. Nodes represent small communities and associated water reservoirs, where the disease can be diffused and grow. The edges reflect the transport of cholera between neighboring communities, due to hydrological flow and human mobility. To localize the source of the outbreak, we monitor 20% of the communities, selected at random (in green). (c) Average distance between the estimated source and the first infected community, vs. the observer density K/N. With 20% of observers, we achieve an average error of less than 4 hops. Note that the first infected community is not necessarily the source of the outbreak, due to the delay between the infection and the actual reporting of the disease. Adapted from Pinto et al. [2012].

close to the average degree—keep in mind that a random network $P(k)$ follows an exponential distribution.

The initial realistic assumptions, a simple diffusion mechanism and an intuitive heuristics yield efficient implementations of their proposal, with $O(N^\alpha)$ complexity (and $\alpha = 3$ for arbitrary graphs).

5.4.2   DYNAMICAL ROLE OF SOURCE AND INTERMEDIATE NODES

A question that has naturally followed from the study of contagious dynamics is where the main spreaders are in the network topology—that is, if the leaders of the process have a specific network position. Beyond who triggers a process, this question aims to spot who can boost it. Marketing experts seek to find those special actors, to engineer the spreading of product adoption [Aral and Walker, 2011, Chen et al., 2010, Kempe et al., 2003]; much in the same way as epidemiologists try to identify the spreaders of a disease, for the opposite reason. These are practical issues which have been tackled on hybrid approaches, where theory and data meet.

To address this question, disease spreading (and especially the SIR model) has become a rather usual benchmark to identify the network features—mainly degree and centrality measures—that perform better when it comes to spotting outstanding spreaders, i.e., the nodes in the network that facilitate larger reach. This is the case of the work by Kitsak and colleagues [Kitsak et al., 2010], for instance. Their work explores whether the degree of a node k or its k-core can help in predicting the spreading capabilities of that node. They modeled the underlying dynamics using the SIR and SIS frameworks, because of the wide range of real-world phenomena they can be mapped onto. The authors' findings indicate that centrality, rather than connectivity, is the key topological feature to understand the spreading power of a node. Besides the untested empirical validity of such a claim, this work triggered a number of efforts to determine which, among centrality descriptors, performed better at spotting influential spreaders. In this vein, Klemm et al. [Klemm et al., 2012], for instance, propose a *dynamical influence* (DI) measure which capitalizes on eigenvector centrality—as opposed to a static, purely topological approach. To demonstrate that DI outperforms k-core centrality's predictions, they used a variety of benchmarks including the SIR scheme and the voter model in opinion dynamics [Castellano et al., 2009].

In a different direction, Borge-Holthoefer and Moreno [Borge-Holthoefer and Moreno, 2012], motivated by the predictions from Kitsak et al. [2010], attempted to identify *super-influencers* in real networks on top of which rumor dynamics were performed (instead of SIR or SIS processes). But surprisingly, the subtle differences between SIR and rumor dynamics suffice to flatten the reported "k-core effect," i.e., rumor outreach and k-core appear to be uncorrelated; see left panel in Figure 5.9. Contrary to the expectations, hubs act as firewalls—they turn stiflers early in the dynamics; see right panel in Figure 5.9—preventing the diffusion of the rumor to large fractions of the underlying structure. We again observe that hubs are key players to constrain the spreading dynamics: they prevent information explosion, and they can prevent information from spreading at all.

These consistent results, obtained by different modeling assumptions, can't explain however why information *does* once in a while actually reach entire communities. Evidence in González-Bailón et al. [2011] and Borge-Holthoefer et al. [2012b], as a matter of fact, suggests that the k-core *is* a good predictor of how far information can get. There are two simple variations on classical rumor models: one is coupling nodes with complex activity patterns [Barabási, 2005] and the other is adding a new transition from ignorant to stifler. Both approaches recover the observed positive centrality-reach correlation [Borge-Holthoefer et al., 2012a]. These stand as examples of how real-world data have already begun to modify idealized setups, launching a converging research avenue for both standpoints toward a sound account of interacting (mis)information dynamics.

The quest for *the* influential spreader still goes on, both on the theoretical and data-driven arenas (and their overlapping region), and most probably there is no unique correct answer [Cheng et al., 2014]: the success of a message may depend on a number of factors which range from the

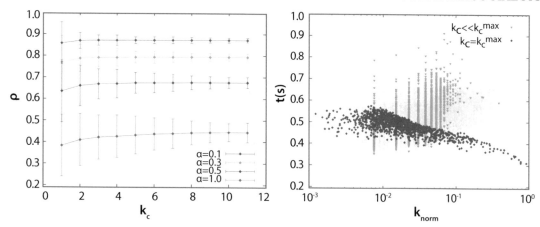

Figure 5.9: Left: Average stifler density ρ for a rumor process triggered at nodes with k-core k_c on an e-mail network. Different spreader-to-stifler probabilities (α) were tested, and yet no correlation is observed between ρ and the source's centrality, i.e., absence of influential spreaders in rumor dynamics. Right: Central nodes (those in k_c^{max}, blue dots) acting as firewalls of the rumor spreading: these nodes are among the first to become stiflers (time-to-stifler $t(s)$ is low), thus acting as topological barriers for the dynamics. For these central nodes, the time it takes them to turn into stiflers is even lower for those with the highest degree (normalized in the x-axis by the k_{max} within a k-shell). The contrast is clear if compared to lower cores (green circles) or, in general, to the rest of the network (gray dots). Adapted from Borge-Holthoefer and Moreno [2012].

medium on which it travels—particular network structure: centrality of the initiator node, but also the features of intermediate nodes [Baños et al., 2013, González-Bailón et al., 2013]—to the inherent properties of the message itself—context, timeliness, truth value, and honesty [Friggeri et al., 2014, Iñiguez et al., 2014], etc.

5.5 MISINFORMATION CONTAINMENT AND MEME MUTATION IN COMPLEX SOCIAL SYSTEMS

We now survey approaches to information mutation and misinformation which rely on minimal modeling assumptions, and turn heavily to algorithmic design and statistical data characterization. Efforts in the line of misinformation containment strongly resemble those—exposed above—regarding rumor source identification (see Section 5.4), both in their assets and limitations. On the other hand, meme extraction and clustering literature has been focused on the technical challenges involved, rather than aiming for a solution in terms of the veracity or quality of the information itself.

5.5.1 INFLUENCE LIMITATION: AVERTING MALICIOUS VIRAL PROCESSES

In August 2013, two Twitter accounts belonging to RIA Novosti state news agency posted reports of the death of former USSR president Mr. Mikhail Gorbachev. The accounts had been hacked into, and started a rumor which evidence—Mr. Gorbachev appeared publicly soon after—brought to a stop.[4] This sort of hoax is all but uncommon in online social media, and their capacity to pervade a population (i.e., to become viral) has been studied: evidence indicates that truth value and honesty *do* matter to increase the probability of a rumor to become global [Friggeri et al., 2014, Iñiguez et al., 2014].

Despite this, some effort has been put to see if a false rumor can be detected and actively stopped. In the context of social networks, the phenomenon of astroturfing,[5] smearing campaigns and misinformation in general has received some attention. An outstanding example of this is Truthy,[6] (see [Ratkiewicz et al., 2011]), an online tool that helps detect the spreading of false rumors on Twitter. Once the data is collected and organized into identifiable memes, Truthy performs a network analysis of the diffusion cascade for each meme. Indeed, even basic structural patterns provide some insight on how *organic* (i.e., natural, legitimate) the diffusion process is, to determine whether it is an instance of genuine information spreading or of astroturfing (with the use of social bots, for instance). In particular, Truthy computes, at the global level, several statistics based on the topology of the largest connected component of the diffusion network, including the number of nodes N and edges L in the graph, the mean degree $\langle k \rangle$ and strength of nodes in the graph, mean edge weight, clustering coefficient, among others. Additionally Truthy tracks—at the node level—the out-degree and out-strength of the most active broadcaster, as well as the in-degree and in-strength of the most focused-upon user. Finally, Truthy also exploits sentiment analysis to determine the mood associated with each meme, using a modified version of the Google-based Profile of Mood States (GPOMS) sentiment analysis method [Bollen et al., 2010].

Regarding the second part (actively bringing false information to a stop), the main strategy to pursue the limitation of a propagating process is to launch the true counter-rumor, and start a competition between two simultaneous cascades. This is, admittedly, a rather naive action to take. The real challenge, however, is to decide which nodes should be "decontaminated" first, i.e., decide who are the optimal source nodes to start the counter-rumor.

This problem—finding the optimal set of nodes to decontaminate, so as to minimize the number of people who adopt the false rumor—has been proved to be NP-hard [Budak et al., 2011]. Here we present an overview of [Nguyen et al., 2012], who devise heuristics under the

---

[4]Sky News, "Gorbachev Forced To Deny Rumors He Is Dead." http://news.sky.com/story/1126199/gorbachev-fo rced-to-deny-rumors-he-is-dead accessed October 2014.

[5]Astroturfing is the use of fake grassroots efforts that primarily focus on influencing public opinion and are typically funded by corporations and governmental entities to form opinions [Cho et al., 2011].

[6]Truthy http://truthy.indiana.edu

assumption that the propagation mechanism is within the family of classic rumor dynamics (independent cascade models). The authors state the problem in the following definition:

Definition 5.1 β_T^I**–Node Protector**. Given a social network represented by a directed graph $G = (V, L)$ and an underlying diffusion model. In the presence of misinformation spreading out on G from either a known or unknown initial set I, the goal is to choose the set $S \subseteq V$ of least nodes to decontaminate with good information so that the expected decontamination ratio on the whole network, after T time windows, is at least β. Here $T \in N$ and $\beta \in [0, 1]$ are input parameters.

Depending on the settings (I: known or unknown; T: constrained or unconstrained), four different variants are developed. Interestingly, the hardest one is that in which I is unknown. For this case, they propose a greedy algorithm which adds nodes having the best marginal influence to the current solution (see Algorithm 5.5.1, from Nguyen et al. [2012]).

Table 5.2: Algorithm adapted from Nguyen et al. [2012]. In it, $|V|$ is the number of nodes in G; $\sigma(v)$ is the expected number of nodes that will be influenced by $v \in V$; and $\sigma(A)$ is the expected number of nodes that will be influenced by $A \subseteq V$.

Algorithm 5.5.1: β-NODE PROTECTOR$(G(V, L), \beta \in (0, 1])$

Initialization
$k \leftarrow 1$
$S_k \leftarrow \emptyset$
repeat
$\quad \begin{cases} v \leftarrow \arg \max\limits_{u \in V \setminus S_k} \{\sigma(S_k + u) - \sigma(S_k)\}; \\ k \leftarrow k + 1; \\ S_k \leftarrow S_k \cup v \end{cases}$
until $\sigma(S_k) > \beta|V|$
return (S)

The authors delve into the variants to Algorithm 5.5.1 for the other three cases, as well as more intricate strategies to ease the cost of the proposal. Its main downside is the extremely slow execution due to the expensive task of estimating the marginal influence when a node is added to the current solution.

For instance, the authors propose to exploit community detection techniques, one of the most prominent research lines in Complex Networks [Fortunato, 2010], so as to exploit a coarse-grained version of the underlying social network. Just as we have highlighted the importance of hubs, there is plenty of evidence of the role communities play in all sorts of dynamics like synchronization [Arenas et al., 2006], transportation [Arenas et al., 2010], or especially information diffusion [Weng et al., 2013]. It turns out that the community-based heuristic algorithm performs competitively—and sometimes better—compared to the original ones, at much lower cost.

5.5.2 INFORMATION MUTATION: MEME TRACKING

In our exposition of the rumor propagation theoretical framework, we have devoted some time to the (very scarce) literature on information explosion, that is, rumor dynamics in which the rumor itself has some mutation probability. Not only is this sort of work hard to find, but also it is not connected to empirical research on the issue. To be precise, there are some works (we will survey a couple of them here) which acknowledge that information mutation happens and try to characterize it—but they do not evaluate their truth value, nor study how resilient the network is in a noisy (therefore less trustworthy) environment.

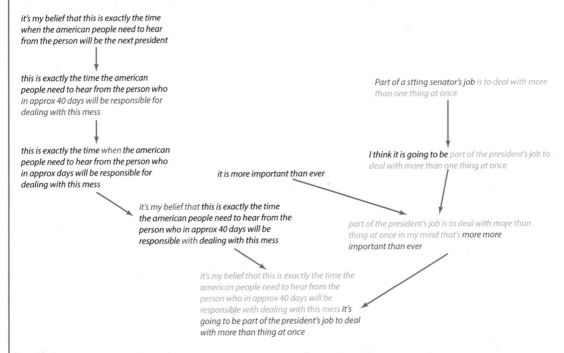

Figure 5.10: A portion of the full set of variants of the quote: "It's going to be a president's job to deal with more than one thing at once." Each box represents a variant of a phrase that appeared on the Web and edges link phrases that share many words. The arrows indicate the (approximate) inclusion of one variant in another. With permission, from http://www.memetracker.org (accessed on December 2014).

In any case, some remarkable lessons can be learned from the empirical approaches to the distortion of information as it travels through digital media. Indeed, it is obvious that social media is facilitating the propagation of memes—but it also enhances their mutation rate: by providing many diffusion channels and flooding individuals with more information than they can actually consume, it creates the right conditions for distortion to happen. Some changes to information are benign, e.g., correcting typos or abbreviating lengthy quotes. But others can change the content's meaning in both intentional and unintentional ways. When mutations occur in this latter form, they raise questions about the authority and reliability of information diffusion through social media, posing a challenge to truth discovery efforts.

We first focus on methodological issues: How can memes be tracked, despite the manifold forms under which it travels? Leskovec et al. [2009]'s approach attempts to identify short distinctive phrases that travel relatively intact through on line text, in a scalable way. The authors are capable of doing so on a massive dataset, providing—at the time of publication—a virtually complete coverage of on line mainstream and blog media.

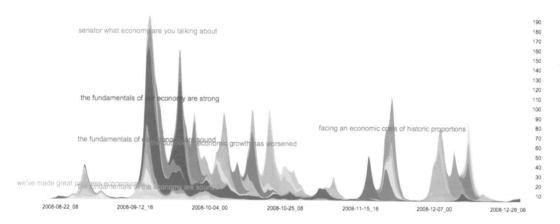

Figure 5.11: Top threads in the news cycle with highest volume for the period Aug. 22–Dec. 28, 2008. Each thread consists of all news articles and blog posts containing a textual variant of economy-related phrases. Phrase variants for the two largest threads in each week are shown as labels pointing to the corresponding thread. The data is drawn as a stacked plot in which the thickness of the strand corresponding to each thread indicates its volume over time. Interactive visualization from `http://www.memetracker.org` (with permission; accessed on December 2014).

The central computational challenge in this approach is to find robust ways of extracting and identifying all the mutational variants of each of these distinctive phrases, and to cluster them together. To do so, the authors develop scalable algorithms for this problem, so that memes end up corresponding to clusters containing all the mutational variants of a single phrase. They proceed in two steps: (i) the construction of a *phrase graph*; and (ii) the community analysis of the resulting graph in such a way that its components will be the phrase clusters.

In the phrase graph, phrases constitute the nodes; an edge (p, q) is added between a pair of phrases p and q such that p is strictly shorter than q, and p has an edit distance to q less than some threshold δ. Given that edges are directed—from shorter to longer phrases—we have a directed acyclic graph (DAG) G at this point. G encodes an approximate inclusion relationship among all the phrases in the data, allowing for small amounts of textual mutation. A weight is also assigned to each edge, defined so that it decreases in the directed edit distance from p to q, and increases in the frequency of q in the corpus. An example of this can be found in Figure 5.10 (see [Leskovec et al., 2009] for details).

The second step is to find a suitable DAG partitioning: given G with edge weights, remove the set of edges of minimum total weight so that each of the resulting components is single-rooted. Such DAG partitioning problem, stated in this way, is NP-hard; so an affordable heuristics is designed to overcome this limitation. The results from this setup are indeed very appealing, since the MemeTracker can successfully spot many "information units" which appear under different shapes. In other words, the output of the MemeTracker scheme is that noisy, apparently manyfold pieces of information can be grouped into topics and tracked across time (see Figure 5.11 and [Leskovec et al., 2009] for details), thus allowing for feasible approaches to truth checking, source detection, etc.

The next step in meme mutation research is taken by Simmons et al. [2011], who—beyond identification—aim to understand how memes change online. To do so, they rely on the afore-mentioned techniques and dataset by Leskovec et al. [2009], and move on looking for mutations in places where they should be occurring the least, namely quoted text, which ought to represent text copied from another source. However, this text can be reframed, by adding to or subtracting from the beginning or end of the quote, or altered with substitutions and omissions. The target of the work is then to quantify the prevalence of changes in memes.

For instance, the authors show that the type and likelihood of change depends on whether the quotation is written on a blog or a mainstream media site, and the popularity of the source that is being copied from. Exploiting the categorization of source type from the MemeTracker dataset (blog or mainstream), the amount of distortion in one or another source can be tracked and quantified. Overall, results indicate—quite surprisingly—that blogs were more likely than mainstream media to copy exact quotes from elsewhere. In other words, there is a slight tendency of mainstream media sources to introduce mutations at a higher rate. This conclusion highlights the fact that the manipulation of a piece of information is context-dependent, with some channels showing larger propensity to mutation than others.

CHAPTER 6

Transdisciplinary Challenges of Truth Discovery

6.1 INTRODUCTION

Truth discovery is a very challenging research topic at the convergence of many disciplines including Data Management, Information Extraction, and Complex Networks as illustrated in Figure 6.1. Previous chapters covered research perspectives and open issues related to each field in isolation. In this concluding chapter, we choose to present the challenges at the intersection of the three disciplines, mainly because we believe that they are the most promising ones but also the most difficult to address. While the challenges we identify hereafter are by no means exhaustive, they refer to certainly important issues to address for designing a truth discovery system and handle the end-to-end pipeline of truth discovery.

6.2 FROM INFORMATION TO DATA

6.2.1 BIG DATA VS. SPARSE FACTS

In many domains, some information sources are more authoritative or specialized, providing accurate information for a small subset of real-world objects, while other sources are generalized with a wider coverage, providing a huge amount of information, some of which may be out-of-date or imprecise. This also refers to the long-tail phenomenon [Li et al., 2014] where most of the sources only provide information about one or few items, and there are only a few sources that provide lots of claims. Determining truth between such sources based only on majority voting and similarity of values can easily lead to erroneous conclusions. Hence, any approach for determining truth needs to consider the possibility that sources have different levels of expertise, various updating policies, and different levels of coverage of information over time. Moreover, similar values across many sources may be due to the likelihood that some information items are either very specific (rare) or very general (popular) and/or sometimes highly correlated; this does not necessarily mean that the sources are dependent but information correlation and distribution have to be analyzed before truth discovery computation. As a very good illustration of this issue, Wikipedia has attracted a large body of research related to automatic quality assessment of Wikipedia articles and trustworthiness estimation of the content [Halfaker et al., 2009]. Intuitively, Wikipedia is reliable for very specialized articles—only contributors who know about a topic dare to edit it; whereas broad, controversial, and "hot" topics are usually not reliable, because

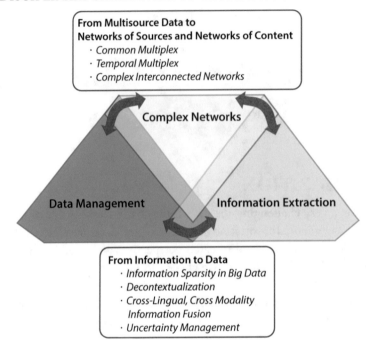

Figure 6.1: Transdisciplinary challenges of truth discovery.

of so many people not agreeing on it and entering into "editorial wars."[1] Typically the length of editors' discussion forums is an indicator of how reliable the article is.

Traditional truth discovery methods presented in Chapter 3 highly depend on the number of conflicts and the number and coverage of the sources. For example, if only one source supports a claim, this claim will be considered to be true or false mainly depending on the reputation and authoritativeness of its single source. If all the sources are independent and agree to support the same claim with no conflict, majority voting will determine that the claim is true because it is supported by the majority. However, in real-world scenarios, the coverage of the information sources follows an exponential distribution, i.e., very few sources provide claims for lots of real-world entities whereas the majority of the remaining sources only cover very few real-world entities (long-tail phenomenon). But it is also the case for the distribution of conflicting values: few data items attract loss of conflicting values whereas other data items will have a value on which most of the sources agree. Hence, despite the availability of Big Data, we may not find enough claims by identified sources providing conflicting information for every fact we want to check.

---

[1]e.g., https://en.wikipedia.org/wiki/Lotka-Volterra_equation vs. https://en.wikipedia.org/wiki/Justin _Bieber

6.2.2   DECONTEXTUALIZATION

When an information item is extracted from its original context and channel, it may lose important "semantic markers" to understand *when, where, how, why,* and *for which* purpose and audience it has been produced, what it is supposed to mean in the absolute sense and also relative to its particular context and information channel. Decontextualization is an inherent part of information extraction and to which extent should be identified and mitigated in truth discovery. Indeed, information without context can be easily distorted, misinterpreted, or misattributed. For example, ascertaining the veracity of controversial information that has been re-tweeted many times in different contexts by various users with different emotions and motivations is a difficult task without the description of these contexts. Moreover, information is updated at a different pace from Twitter, Facebook, and Wikipedia and from sources that have a different granularity (i.e., a source can be an individual, an organization, a company, a government, etc.). Extraction of information from social media content is known to be challenging because texts are typically very short (e.g., 140 characters for Twitter) and noisy (e.g., misspellings, grammatically incorrect sentences, abbreviations, neologisms, and non-ASCII characters). The reliability of the information contained in these messages is also very uncertain when the sources are not authoritative.

Much research has studied the formalization of contexts, and rich context representations have been proposed [Bao et al., 2010]. However, current information extraction methods constrain the context representation and can usually not handle a wide, unpredictable range of topics and they usually do not handle media platform's constraints and specificities over the content generation.

Ultimately, all meta-information about the context, information sources' characteristics, and content channel constraints have to be filtered and encoded, so some can be analyzed and used as evidence for truth discovery.

Over the last decade, statistical sequence labeling models and especially Conditional Random Fields (CRFs) [Lafferty et al., 2001] have become the dominant technique for information extraction tasks. In many scenarios, the entities or relationships in textual data are not independent and identically distributed; they depend on the information production and communication contexts. For truth discovery, we need to capture contextual evidence and information lineage to go beyond current collective information extraction approaches [Klügl et al., 2012]. A major challenge is to implement context inference and semantic recontextualization possibility with adapting computational linguistics theory (See Chapter 7 of Saeed [2009]).

When contextual evidence is missing, a dual challenge is to detect the cases where information has been selectively excerpted from its original context in a way that has distorted the source's intended meaning. This practice (commonly referred to as "quoting out of context" or as "contextomy") can seriously impair information extraction and by-product the truth discovery results and constitutes by itself a challenging research topic.

6.2.3   UNCERTAIN, INCOMPLETE, AND BIASED OBSERVATIONS

Observation data may be incomplete and biased for various reasons: some information sources may not give all their data for security or privacy concerns; some sources have format limitations; when the sources do not explicitly provide temporal or spatial information, the time and location values are missing and need to be inferred.

Typically, the Open World assumption holds since not all the real-world entities/events may have been observed and reported by identified sources.

We have various levels of *a priori* knowledge on how the observation data have been collected from online sources. In many cases of social sensing, opportunistic (or volunteered) data can be *biased by observation effort* and the underlying observation method is usually unknown. It is thus important to explore how one can retrieve and quantify the observation effort from modeling the distribution of data providers/observers particularly in social and crowd-sourcing applications. Data can be biased in many other ways. For example, data can be affected by a *selection bias* that is the extent to which a piece of information is claimed by a category of individuals (e.g., experts in Pal et al. [2012]) who are likely to have access to or knowledge of a certain type of media or channel they choose to use.[2] Data may also suffer from the *observer's bias*—related to the individual's ability to accurately remember and describe events—and *disclosure bias*—related to a witness's incentive (or disincentive) to include certain events or details. One critical challenge is to estimate the whole range of uncertainties, incompleteness, and biases from the observers to the information extraction and fact-checking modules and take them into account in the truth discovery computation.

6.2.4   DATA AND INFORMATION FUSION ACROSS LANGUAGES, MODALITIES, AND MEDIA

The agility of a truth discovery system is of utmost importance at the technical, structural, and semantic levels. Agility can be defined as the ability of the system to efficiently extract and map information from various languages, in various formats and data structures, supported by various media, and disseminated through various channels (e.g., Twitter, Instagram, YouTube, etc.). Traditional information extraction pipelines require several analysis stages ranging from text preprocessing to coreference and entity resolution. For each document, once entities, attributes, and relations are recognized and extracted, statements are identified, and sentences, they have to be linked across multiple pieces of content in different languages to be classified (e.g., as a rumor or a fact). A number of applications have been deployed for information extraction as discussed in Chapter 2, but most of them use hand-crafted lists of terms and regular expressions, rather than corpus-trained approaches. They are usually specific to a single channel/application/language (e.g., English) and cannot be considered "agile" enough for extracting, gathering, and aligning in-

---

[2]E.g., social media users are usually younger, technologically savvy, motivated individuals vs. individuals who are older, more remote, lacking access or ability or motivation to use technology and whose stories/observations are likely missing from this channel.

formation from various languages, formats, or channels. Moreover, each stage of textual content analysis (from preprocessing, entity matching, to classification) produces systematic and random errors that need to be considered in truth discovery computation. None of the very few attempts to couple these applications to truth discovery systems (e.g., [Goasdoué et al., 2013]) has considered the uncertainty resulting from the information extraction process which affects the truth discovery results. Tracing and estimating the errors of information extraction, formatting, and linking is one of the main challenges in truth discovery from unstructured content.

The research challenges discussed so far in previous chapters were mainly concerned with structured and textual data. But various user-generated content is available as a blend of texts, audio recordings, images, and videos. State-of-the-art techniques for extracting and fusing information are facing new challenges of dealing with large-scale heterogeneous data sources providing content in various medias, languages, and modalities. For example, a Web news page about "Sharks after Hurricane Katrina" is composed by text describing the event (e.g., " Mayor Aaron Broussard of Jefferson Parish (a New Orleans suburb), who, according to the Aug. 30, 2005 issue of the Palm Beach Post, told residents that at least one 3-foot shark had been spotted"), images (e.g., images about the disaster), and videos (e.g., a shark swimming on a flooded street) containing additional information regarding the real extent of the event or providing evidence corroborating the text part.

The main challenge of cross-modality information fusion for truth discovery is first to exploit information across different parts of multimedia documents and link them via cross-media coreference resolution. The goal is to handle multimedia information by considering not only the document's text and image data but also the layout structure which determines how a given text block is related to a particular image or video. This requires a great deal of new developments beyond ontology definition, data annotation, image, audio, and video processing. An overview on the challenges in information extraction, in particular addressing cross-document, cross-lingual, and cross-media information extraction and fusion may be found in Ji [2010]. We are at the very beginning of the next exciting research avenue on cross-modality truth discovery.

6.3   FROM MULTISOURCE DATA TO NETWORKS OF SOURCES AND NETWORKS OF CONTENT

The main limitation of the approaches outlined in Chapter 5 is, undoubtedly, its level of simplification. While the ideas deployed there capture much of the complexity of information dynamics *on a single network* ("monoplex"), they render a somewhat naive account of real world phenomena. Indeed, online social interaction, for instance, does not usually happen in a single dimension (say, exclusively on Twitter), but rather in a multi-layered information ecosystem. For instance, the notice about a certain YouTube video reaches a friend of ours on Tumblr, who then simultaneously diffuses it through Twitter and Facebook—while, later on, somebody might share it via email. With this everyday example we have already overrun the "standard" approach, which can only explain the diffusion of (mis)information over a single layer.

Networked systems that cannot be represented as traditional graphs have already been studied from a data-mining perspective. For example, heterogeneous networks were developed as a framework to accommodate multiple types of nodes and edges [Sun and Han, 2013]. Similarly, meta-matrices are used in dynamic network analysis [Carley, 2003], which can incorporate spatiotemporal information, different node types and attributes, as well as other types of data about social networks within the same framework. Indeed, examples are numerous. A shortcoming of these approaches, however, is their lack of attention to dynamical processes (or, equivalently, their attention solely to structural matters). As we have seen in Chapter 5, the structure of a network (i.e., its "building features" and statistical characterization) is important inasmuch it affects and constrains its information dynamics happening *on top of* it, be it epidemic spreading or information diffusion. Comparably, advances in non-standard network analysis are useful, but they render an incomplete (and often an *ad hoc*) account of the phenomena happening in the network.

We thus foresee the need for a "multiplex" update: as research on complex systems has matured, it has become essential to move beyond simple graphs and investigate more complicated but more realistic frameworks. At first sight, the expansion from monoplex to multiplex may be hailed as an easy one—instead of a network of agents with their corresponding interactions, we now have a stack of networks with the same agents, and different interactions: an individual's persona on Twitter, Facebook, etc., plus the relationships she holds on each of those. Each node at one level is connected to itself in the next level, and that pretty much suffices. However, things turn out to be more complicated. Achieving a deep understanding of such systems calls for the generalization of "traditional" network theory, developing a more powerful mathematical framework to cope with the challenges posed by multilayer complex systems [De Domenico et al., 2013]. To begin with, an adjacency matrix can no longer encode the subtleties of multiplexed systems, and rather *adjacency tensors* [Dunlavy et al., 2011, Kolda and Bader, 2009, Sun et al., 2006a] need to enter the scene. This in turn modifies all the underlying algebra, which is at the base of monoplex network analysis (see Chapter 5). This section is not the place to introduce the tensorial framework to study multilayer networks, or to discuss the generalization of network descriptors and dynamical processes—degree, transitivity, eigenvector centrality, modularity, etc.—which the reader can find elsewhere [De Domenico et al., 2014a, Kivelä et al., 2014]. It is rather the opportunity to point out future challenges (thus, potential research niches) that lie ahead in the new multiplex arena, which is itself still under construction. To limit the scope in the following, we will only consider a few (out of the manifold combinations, see Table 1 in Kivelä et al. [2014]) multi-layered systems.

(1) Common multiplex: Any node i can belong to any of the layers. Edges can only exist between different nodes in the same layer, i.e. edges across layers only connect nodes with themselves in all the layers where it exists. Layers correspond to different *aspects* or dimensions of interaction (in the aforementioned example, the fact that we may interact online via

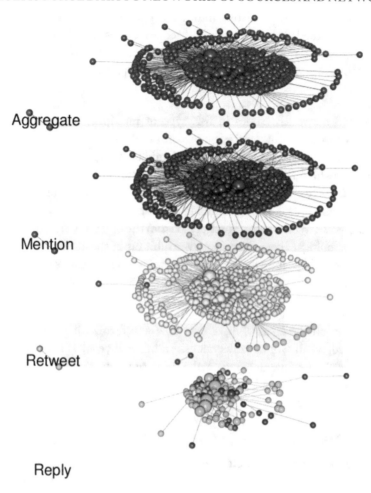

Aggregate

Mention

Retweet

Reply

Figure 6.2: A Twitter multiplex: each layer represents a distinct information diffusion dynamics (via mentions, re-tweets, or replies), such that the nodes (users) are repeated across layers—but different links are drawn, depending on the activity they had. Note that a node may not be in every layer, if it did not show activity there. The uppermost layer aggregates the other three, highlighting how different phenomena are observed if a monoplexed or a multiplexed view is chosen. The figure has been obtained with the freely available MuxViz software,[3] for the analysis and visualization of multiplex networks.

different platforms), and no time evolution is considered. This type of multiplex corresponds to the representation in Figure 6.2.

[3]http://muxviz.net, accessed on June 2015.

(2) Temporal multiplex: Layers in this multiplex represent time. Again, any node i can be present in any of the layers, but cross-layer edges are restricted to those immediately preceding or succeeding them [Mucha et al., 2010]. Formally, this means that layers can be mapped to times $t, t + \Delta t, t + 2\Delta t, \ldots$ in a rigid sequence. See Figure 6.3 for an illustration.

(3) Interconnected networks: Nodes in this type of multiplex can only exist in one of the layers, representing the (otherwise quite common) situation in which different systems $(\alpha, \beta, \ldots, M)$ interact in complex ways. A familiar example of this is transportation systems in cities, where different networks are interconnected: a citizen can travel on the road network, switch to the subway system, and later take a bus to her final destination [De Domenico et al., 2014b]. Similarly, a rumor will be disseminated through a video on YouTube, as re-tweeted pictures extracted from the original video, textual comments, and analysis in microblogs. These systems may exhibit (as in the example) any number of layers but, given our focus on information systems, we will restrict ourselves to $M = 2$ (source-content interconnected network). Figure 6.2 illustrates such systems which additionally can evolve in time.

Noteworthy, in all three cases, links may take any form, with weighted or unweighted, directed or undirected, positive or negative values. Additionally, each single slice in (1) and (2) may be unipartite or bipartite—while in (3) we make the case for an extension of bipartite networks, in which across-layer links represent inter-class relations, while within-layer links represent intra-class connections.

6.3.1   TRUTH DISCOVERY IN COMMON MULTIPLEXES

Our online experience is inherently heterogeneous with regard to the format in which (and the platforms where) information is delivered to us. We also begin to have a certain knowledge of how such multiplexed systems grow—how links are formed at each new layer—both empirically [Lee and Monge, 2011] and theoretically [Klimek and Thurner, 2013]. We ignore, however, whether (and how) such a multi-platform environment facilitates information spreading (which of course includes false rumors, noisy and/or inexact facts, etc.).

Research has already tackled this question, at least at a theoretical (and admittedly idealized) level. For instance, analytical and numerical results in Brummitt et al. [2012] deliver evidence that a multiplexed scenario increases the vulnerability of global cascades, provided we adapt Watts's threshold-cascades model [Borge-Holthoefer et al., 2013, Watts, 2002]. This implies that multiplexity offers a feasible tactic to boost (or hinder) large-scale information diffusion by introducing or removing layers, respectively. From another perspective, Gómez et al. [Gómez et al., 2013] find that the multiplex structure is able to speed up the less diffusive of the layers in a set of interconnected networks, as revealed by the structure of eigenvectors and eigenvalues of the complete network in terms of the spectral properties of the individual layers. Other questions of interest may be those of epidemic spreading [Sanz et al., 2014] and percolation processes (structural fragility) [Bashan et al., 2013, Cellai et al., 2013] on such networks, given their close connection to information dynamics.

We don't have, however, the observational counterparts of those outcomes in real life. Indeed, research here faces two difficult technical problems.

First, it is true that we are now endowed with large amounts of publicly available data, thanks to a collection of APIs which eases our access to online records. And yet, it is not easy to identify users across multiple social platforms [Ferrara et al., 2014, Vosecky et al., 2009]. This makes it hard to conduct experiments in real settings. A possible line of research should exploit the potentialities of partial information: given that *some* individuals can be identified in different platforms, whereas some nodes may remain untagged, techniques for link prediction/inference can be exploited to solve this [Guimerà and Sales-Pardo, 2009, Lü and Zhou, 2011].

Second, it is not obvious that two pieces of information, delivered in different formats, actually refer to the same thing or idea—this latter problem points again to the need for data and information fusion techniques, i.e., fusion methods to reliably reduce different versions and formats of information to a single, "normalized" representation (see Section 6.2.4 above).

6.3.2   TIME-DEPENDENT TRUTH DISCOVERY

Discovering truth from past events and historical data is certainly useful, and results may be validated more easily since ground truth and full data sets already exist before the time of analysis. However, from a humanitarian perspective for example, actionable truth discovery from quasi real-time data could save lives. In this context, information extraction as well as truth discovery computation need to be streamlined, prioritized, and adjusted to the degree of emergency and incompleteness of available information. This important usage-driven aspect goes beyond consistency and constraints checking. For example, information such as "The Chrysler building had an explosion and it affected the Empire State building" can be automatically verified: these buildings are about 2 km away and hence this information cannot be true. However, more often what journalists/emergency responders need is to verify information such as "The Chrysler building had an explosion" when there are very few primary sources claiming it initially. After some time, more sources will cover the event, adding more information or external evidence confirming or refuting previous claims as time passes. Timely and actionable truth discovery requires the prioritization and adjustment of information checking tasks specifically to the communities that will use the data. Previous work presented in Chapter 3 on truth discovery mainly focus on static databases although recent advances address truth discovery from continuous data streams [Zhao et al., 2014] and evolving truth [Dong et al., 2009b, Li et al., 2015b]. Recent advances in mobile technologies have led to various online data intensive applications, where large volumes of data streams are being collected continuously. Such high-speed incoming stream data makes it impractical to make multiple passes of the data for truth discovery, while it is also unrealistic to assume that the data can be loaded into main memory for truth discovery. For applications such as disaster responses or journalism, short response time is a critical requirement, not only from a technical and application-dependent perspective but also to capture the inherent evolving nature of (our knowledge of) the truth.

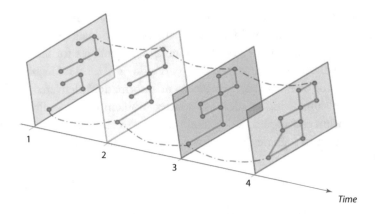

Figure 6.3: Temporal multiplex: each layer represents a different snapshot, capturing the rewiring of a network at discrete times $t = \{1, 2, 3, 4\}$ (arbitrary units). Inter-layer connections exist only between adjacent slices.

The problems that stem from the inclusion of the temporal dimension in networks have been well-known for over a decade [Kempe et al., 2000]. We have already seen in Chapter 5 that, as agents in a networked system communicate over time, information flows in complex ways; *time-respecting* paths are crucial, as we have seen in the problem of source identification. These difficulties increase if we now consider two different, co-existing dynamics: that of the information flow, and that of a *temporally evolving* structure, in which link addition, deletion, and rewiring is possible. Indeed, to put it in context, the social networks on which information is flowing is constantly changing: users start and cease to follow peers on Twitter; friending and un-friending dynamics occur constantly on Facebook. Admittedly, this is not a serious constraint to understand information flow (or epidemics, or any other diffusing process) when both dynamics have radically different—very fast, very slow—time-scales [Holme and Saramäki, 2012, Vespignani, 2012]. For instance, viral cascades occur in the range from minutes to days; whereas substantial change in the following-follower Twitter network may be happening in rather slow time-scales, i.e., weeks to months. In such cases, any study that intends to tackle information flow can safely disregard structural dynamics, which can then be considered static.

That is not the case, however, during certain events of emergency or social unrest. Under these particular circumstances, rewiring and/or network disruption may occur at rapid timescales—fast enough so as to affect diffusion dynamics. This particular setting has been at the center of the focus in temporal networks research, highlighting how the dynamical properties of information flow in monoplex networks are perturbed under fast structural change. Again—as it has been the case for many examples before—the accent is placed on theoretical settings [Perra et al., 2012, Ribeiro et al., 2013, Starnini et al., 2012], leaving aside actual applications.

6.3.3   COMPLEX INTERCONNECTED NETWORKS OF SOURCES AND MULTIMEDIA CONTENT

The third highlighted multiplex is that of interconnected networks which additionally evolve in time as illustrated in Figure 6.4. This highly complex scenario, with disjoint sets of nodes on each layer, intra, and inter-layer connections, and temporal resolution is—to the best of our knowledge—unexplored so far, both at the theoretical and empirical levels. One step behind, in terms of complexity, we find the work of Borge-Holthoefer et al. [2015] which incorporates the existence of node classes and temporal evolution—but not intra-layer connections. The latter reduces such work to the case of a temporal bipartite multiplex (that is, the previous section with the bipartite addition).

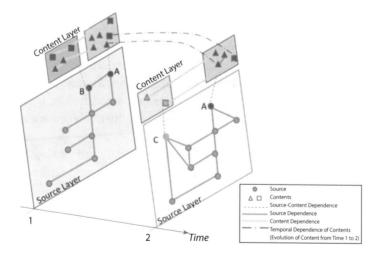

Figure 6.4: Complex interconnected networks: For two snapshots at different times, two layers represent respectively the source network (e.g., Twitter users) and the content network. Inter-layer connections (or dependencies) exist between the sources, between their content sharing at each given time, and also across time since content may change, mutate, disappear, or have cross-references. Similarly a source node can disappear (B) and a new source can appear (C) in the time interval and sources may be implicitly and/or explicitly dependent.

Such work, which pivots on real data from Twitter, applies an ecosystems approach to prove the cooperative-competitive nature of source-content systems. The authors in Borge-Holthoefer et al. [2015] find that consensus (the survival of certain pieces of content vs. the extinction of others) around a topic builds up in time, showing some architectural signatures (i.e., network structural patterns) which change as consensus is reached: in the developmental stages, a topic (understood here as some users generating a number of pieces of related content) exhibit a sparse and modular structure, i.e., many small clusters, with limited or no interaction among them, start generating similar content. In the mature phases, however, clusters become fuzzy and the system converges toward a dominantly nested structure [Bascompte et al., 2003], where some users and pieces of content become *generalists* (for instance, a #hashtag used by a large subset of users), whereas some remain specialists.

All of this suggests that we confront very complex modes of interaction, in which indirect connections (for instance, the fact that two users share similar content despite the fact that they do not interact directly) may shape new forms of influence and content diffusion, at different layers and across time. It remains a challenge to cope with all the ingredients at a time, in a reliable and efficient manner.

6.4   FINAL REMARK

The quest for automating truth discovery and reliable fact-checking is at its initial stages. As soon as the social data deluge arrived, the technical (algorithmic, efficiency-sensitive) challenges have been complemented with structural and dynamical ones: it is not possible anymore to discuss the origin of a hoax, unless diffusion mechanisms are understood. Solutions, we envisage, will not come from a single discipline but rather from the intersection of many. These include information extraction from various media, data management, curation and fusion, trust management, and complex network modeling to capture the multiplexed, multi-modal, temporally evolving nature of information diffusion in the Web 2.0.

As such, this book does—hopefully—lay out an initial draft of how these different communities could converge to evaluate the veracity of Big Data—and find truth needles in noisy haystacks.

Bibliography

Lada Adamic. The small world Web. *Research and Advanced Technology for Digital Libraries*, pages 852–852, 1999. DOI: 10.1007/3-540-48155-9_27. 82

Ameya Agaskar and Yue M. Lu. A fast Monte Carlo algorithm for source localization on graphs. In *SPIE Optical Engineering + Applications*, pages 88581N–88581N. International Society for Optics and Photonics, 2013. DOI: 10.1117/12.2023039. 94

Eugene Agichtein and Luis Gravano. Snowball: Extracting relations from large plain-text collections. In *Proceedings of the Fifth ACM Conference on Digital Libraries (DL'00)*, pages 85–94, 2000. DOI: 10.1145/336597.336644. 15, 21

Gabor Angeli, Arun Tejasvi Chaganty, Angel X. Chang, Kevin Reschke, Julie Tibshirani, Jean Wu, Osbert Bastani, Keith Siilats, and Christopher D. Manning. Stanford's 2013 KBP system. In *Proceedings of the Sixth Text Analysis Conference (TAC 2013)*, 2013. 24

Gabor Angeli, Julie Tibshirani, Jean Wu, and Christopher D. Manning. Combining distant and partial supervision for relation extraction. In *Proceedings of the 2014 Conference on Empirical Methods in Natural Language Processing (EMNLP 2014)*, pages 1556–1567, 2014. DOI: 10.3115/v1/D14-1164. 24, 25

Sinan Aral and Dylan Walker. Creating social contagion through viral product design: a randomized trial of peer influence in networks. *Management Science*, 57.9:1623–1639, 2011. DOI: 10.1287/mnsc.1110.1421. 95

Alex Arenas, Albert Díaz-Guilera, and Conrad J. Pérez-Vicente. Synchronization reveals topological scales in complex networks. *Physical Review Letters*, 96(11):114102, 2006. DOI: 10.1103/PhysRevLett.96.114102. 100

Alex Arenas, Javier Borge-Holthoefer, Sergio Gómez, and Gorka Zamora-López. Optimal map of the modular structure of complex networks. *New Journal of Physics*, 12:053009, 2010. DOI: 10.1088/1367-2630/12/5/053009. 100

Raquel A. Baños, Javier Borge-Holthoefer, and Yamir Moreno. The role of hidden influentials in the diffusion of online information cascades. *EPJ Data Science*, 2(6), 2013. DOI: 10.1140/epjds18. 88, 97

Norman T. J. Bailey and Larry Bailey. *The mathematical theory of infectious diseases and its applications*. Charles Griffin & Company Ltd, 2 edition, 1975. 87

Raju Balakrishnan and Subbarao Kambhampati. SourceRank: Relevance and trust assessment for deep Web sources based on inter-source agreement. In *Proceedings of 20th International World Wide Web Conference (WWW 2011)*, March/April 2011. 42

Krisztian Balog, Pavel Serdyukov, and Arjen P. de Vries. Overview of the TREC 2010 entity track. In *Proceedings of the Nineteenth Text REtrieval Conference (TREC 2010)*, 2010. 16

Michele Banko, Michael J. Cafarella, Stephen Soderland, Matt Broadhead, and Oren Etzioni. Open information extraction from the Web. In *Proceedings of the 20th International Joint Conference on Artificial Intelligence (IJCAI'07)*, pages 2670–2676, 2007. DOI: 10.1145/1409360.1409378. 22, 28

Nikhil Bansal, Avrim Blum, and Shuchi Chawla. Correlation clustering. *Mach. Learn.*, 56(1-3): 89–113, June 2004. DOI: 10.1023/B:MACH.0000033116.57574.95. 18

Jie Bao, Jiao Tao, Deborah L. McGuinness, and Paul Smart. Context representation for the semantic Web. In *Proceedings of the Web Science Conference*, Raleigh, USA, 2010. 105

A. Lazlo Barabási. The origin of bursts and heavy tails in human dynamics. *Nature*, 435(7063): 1251–1251, 2005. DOI: 10.1038/nature03459. 96

A.Lazlo Barabási and Reka Albert. Emergence of scaling in random networks. *Science*, 286:509, 1999. DOI: 10.1126/science.286.5439.509. 79, 86

Denilson Barbosa, Haixun Wang, and Cong Yu. Inferencing in information extraction: Techniques and applications (tutorial). In *Proceedings of the 31st IEEE International Conference on Data Engineering, (ICDE 2015)*, pages 1534–1537, 2015. DOI: 10.1109/ICDE.2015.7113420. 11

Alain Barrat, Marc Barthélemy, and Alessandro Vespignani. *Dynamical processes on complex networks*. Cambridge University Press, New York, NY, USA, 2008. DOI: 10.1017/CBO9780511791383. 77

Jordi Bascompte, Pedro Jordano, Carlos J Melián, and Jens M Olesen. The nested assembly of plant–animal mutualistic networks. *Proceedings of the National Academy of Sciences*, 100(16): 9383–9387, 2003. DOI: 10.1073/pnas.1633576100. 114

Amir Bashan, Yehiel Berezin, Sergey V. Buldyrev, and Shlomo Havlin. The extreme vulnerability of interdependent spatially embedded networks. *Nature Physics*, 9(10):667–672, 2013. DOI: 10.1038/nphys2727. 111

Carlo Batini and Monica Scannapieco. *Data Quality: Concepts, Methodologies and Techniques (Data-Centric Systems and Applications)*. Springer-Verlag, Secaucus, NJ, USA, 2006. ISBN 3540331727. DOI: 10.1007/3-540-33173-5. 1

Abraham Berman and Robert J. Plemmons. Nonnegative matrices. *SIAM Classics in Applied Mathematics,*, 9, 1979. 82

Laure Berti-Equille. Measuring and modelling data quality for quality-awareness in data mining. In *Quality Measures in Data Mining*, pages 101–126. 2007a. DOI: 10.1007/978-3-540-44918-8_5. 1

Laure Berti-Equille. Habilitation a Diriger des Recherches. University of Rennes 1, France, 2007b. 1

Laure Berti-Equille and Javier Borge-Holthoefer. Veracity of big data: From truth discovery computation algorithms to models of misinformation dynamics (tutorial). In *Proceedings of the 24th ACM International on Conference on Information and Knowledge Management, (CIKM 2015)*, 2015. 2

Laure Berti-Equille, Tamraparni Dasu, and Divesh Srivastava. Discovery of complex glitch patterns: A novel approach to quantitative data cleaning. In *Proceedings of the 27th International Conference on Data Engineering, (ICDE 2011)*, pages 733–744, 2011. DOI: 10.1109/ICDE.2011.5767864. 3

Laure Berti-Equille, Ji Meng Loh, and Tamraparni Dasu. A masking index for quantifying hidden glitches. *Knowl. Inf. Syst.*, 44(2):253–277, 2015. DOI: 10.1007/s10115-014-0760-0. 3

Elisa Bertino, Chenyun Dai, and Murat Kantarcioglu. The challenge of assuring data trustworthiness. In *Proceedings of the 14th International Conference on Database Systems for Advanced Applications, (DASFAA 2009)*, pages 22–33, 2009. DOI: 10.1007/978-3-642-00887-0_2. 1

Daniel M. Bikel, Richard Schwartz, and Ralph M. Weischedel. An algorithm that learns what's in a name. *Mach. Learn.*, 34(1-3):211–231, February 1999. DOI: 10.1023/A:1007558221122. 15, 18

Vangelis G. Bintzios, Thanasis G. Papaioannou, , and George D. Stamoulis. An effective approach for accurate estimation of trust of distant information sources in the semantic Web. In *Proceedings of the Second International Workshop on Security, Privacy and Trust in Pervasive and Ubiquitous Computing, (SecPerU 2006)*, 2006. DOI: 10.1109/SECPERU.2006.4. 73

Lorenzo Blanco, Valter Crescenzi, Paolo Merialdo, and Paolo Papotti. Probabilistic models to reconcile complex data from inaccurate data sources. In *Advanced Information Systems Engineering*, volume 6051 of *Lecture Notes in Computer Science*, pages 83–97, 2010. DOI: 10.1007/978-3-642-13094-6_8. 41

Stefano Boccaletti, Vito Latora, Yamir Moreno, Mario Chavez, and Dong-Uk Hwang. Complex networks: Structure and dynamics. *Physics Reports*, 424(4-5):175–308, 2006. DOI: 10.1016/j.physrep.2005.10.009. 77

Johan Bollen, Huina Mao, and Alberto Pepe. Determining the public mood state by analysis of microblogging posts. In *Proceedings of the Alife XII Conference*, pages 667–668, 2010. 98

Béla Bollobás. *Random Graphs*. Academic Press, New York, 2nd edition, 2001. 83

Philip Bonacich. Factoring and weighting approaches to status scores and clique identification. *Journal of Mathematical Sociology*, 2(1):113–120, 1972. DOI: 10.1080/0022250X.1972.9989806. 81

Kalina Bontcheva, Leon Derczynski, Adam Funk, Mark Greenwood, Diana Maynard, and Niraj Aswani. TwitIE: An open-source information extraction pipeline for microblog text. In *Proceedings of the International Conference on Recent Advances in Natural Language Processing*, 2013. 11

Javier Borge-Holthoefer and Yamir Moreno. Absence of influential spreaders in rumor dynamics. *Physical Review E*, 85:026116, 2012. DOI: 10.1103/PhysRevE.85.026116. 8, 96, 97

Javier Borge-Holthoefer, Sandro Meloni, Bruno Gonçalves, and Yamir Moreno. Emergence of influential spreaders in modified rumor models. *Journal of Statistical Physics*, 148(6):1–11, 2012a. DOI: 10.1007/s10955-012-0595-6. 96

Javier Borge-Holthoefer, Alejandro Rivero, and Yamir Moreno. Locating privileged spreaders on an online social network. *Physical Review E*, 85:066123, 2012b. DOI: 10.1103/PhysRevE.85.066123. 96

Javier Borge-Holthoefer, Raquel A. Baños, Sandra González-Bailón, and Yamir Moreno. Cascading behaviour in complex socio-technical networks. *Journal of Complex Networks*, 1(1):3–24, 2013. DOI: 10.1093/comnet/cnt006. 110

Javier Borge-Holthoefer, Raquel A. Baños, Carlos Gracia-Lázaro, and Yamir Moreno. The nested assembly of collective attention in online social systems. *arXiv preprint arXiv:1501.06809*, 2015. 113, 114

Léon Bottou. On-line learning in neural networks. Chapter in On-line Learning and Stochastic Approximations, pages 9–42. 1998. 59

Ulrik Brandes. A faster algorithm for betweenness centrality. *Journal of Mathematical Sociology*, 25(2):163–177, 2001. DOI: 10.1080/0022250X.2001.9990249. 81

Sergey Brin and Lawrence Page. The anatomy of a large-scale hypertextual web search engine. *Computer Networks*, 30(1-7):107–117, 1998. DOI: 10.1016/S0169-7552(98)00110-X. 42

Charles D. Brummitt, Kyu-Min Lee, and K-I Goh. Multiplexity-facilitated cascades in networks. *Physical Review E*, 85(4):045102, 2012. DOI: 10.1103/PhysRevE.85.045102. 110

Ceren Budak, Divyakant Agrawal, and Amr El Abbadi. Limiting the spread of misinformation in social networks. In *Proceedings of the 20th International Conference on World Wide Web (WWW 2011)*, pages 665–674, 2011. DOI: 10.1145/1963405.1963499. 98

Razvan C. Bunescu and Raymond J. Mooney. A shortest path dependency kernel for relation extraction. In *Proceedings of the Conference on Human Language Technology and Empirical Methods in Natural Language Processing (HLT'05)*, pages 724–731, 2005a. DOI: 10.3115/1220575.1220666. 21, 22

Razvan C. Bunescu and Raymond J. Mooney. Subsequence kernels for relation extraction. In *Advances in Neural Information Processing Systems 18, (NIPS 2005)*, pages 171–178, 2005b. 21, 22

Razvan C. Bunescu and Marius Pasca. Using encyclopedic knowledge for named entity disambiguation. In *Proceedings of the 11th Conference of the European Chapter of the Association for Computational Linguistics (EACL 2006)*, 2006. 20

Guido Caldarelli. *Scale-free networks: Complex Webs in nature and technology*. Oxford University Press, USA, 2007. 77

Kathleen M. Carley. Dynamic network analysis. In *Dynamic Social Network Modeling and Analysis: Workshop Summary and Papers, Committee on Human Factors, National Research Council, National Research Council*, pages 133–145, 2003. 108

Taylor Cassidy, Heng Ji, Hongbo Deng, Jing Zheng, and Jiawei Han. Analysis and refinement of cross-lingual entity linking. In *Proceedings of the Third International Conference of the CLEF Initiative*, pages 1–12, 2012. DOI: 10.1007/978-3-642-33247-0_1. 19

Claudio Castellano, Santo Fortunato, and Vittorio Loreto. Statistical physics of social dynamics. *Reviews of Modern Physics*, 81(2):591, 2009. DOI: 10.1103/RevModPhys.81.591. 96

Davide Cellai, Eduardo López, Jie Zhou, James P. Gleeson, and Ginestra Bianconi. Percolation in multiplex networks with overlap. *Physical Review E*, 88(5):052811, 2013. DOI: 10.1103/PhysRevE.88.052811. 111

Chia-Hui Chang, Mohammed Kayed, Moheb Ramzy Girgis, and Khaled F. Shaalan. A survey of Web information extraction systems. *IEEE Trans. on Knowl. and Data Eng.*, 18(10):1411–1428, October 2006. DOI: 10.1109/TKDE.2006.152. 11

Wei Chen, Chi Wang, and Yajun Wang. Scalable influence maximization for prevalent viral marketing in large-scale social networks. In *Proceedings of the 16th ACM SIGKDD International Conference on Knowledge Discovery and Data mining*, pages 1029–1038, 2010. DOI: 10.1145/1835804.1835934. 95

Justin Cheng, Lada Adamic, P. Alex Dow, Jon Michael Kleinberg, and Jure Leskovec. Can cascades be predicted? In *Proceedings of the 23rd International Conference on World Wide Web (WWW 2014)*, pages 925–936, 2014. DOI: 10.1145/2566486.2567997. 96

Xiao Cheng and Dan Roth. Relational inference for Wikification. In *Proceedings of the 2013 Conference on Empirical Methods in Natural Language Processing (EMNLP 2013)*, pages 1787–1796, 2013. 21

Charles H. Cho, Martin L. Martens, Hakkyun Kim, and Michelle Rodrigue. Astroturfing global warming: It isn't always greener on the other side of the fence. *Journal of Business Ethics*, 104 (4):571–587, 2011. DOI: 10.1007/s10551-011-0950-6. 98

Peter Christen. A survey of indexing techniques for scalable record linkage and deduplication. *IEEE Trans. on Knowl. and Data Eng.*, 24(9):1537–1555, September 2012. DOI: 10.1109/TKDE.2011.127. 19

Sarah Cohen, James T. Hamilton, and Fred Turner. Computational journalism. *Commun. ACM*, 54(10):66–71, October 2011a. DOI: 10.1145/2001269.2001288. 63

Sarah Cohen, Chengkai Li, Jun Yang, and Cong Yu. Computational journalism: A call to arms to database researchers. In *Proceedings of the Fifth Biennial Conference on Innovative Data Systems Research (CIDR 2011)*, pages 148–151, 2011b. 29

Cleo Condoravdi, Dick Crouch, Valeria de Paiva, Reinhard Stolle, and Daniel G. Bobrow. Entailment, intensionality and text understanding. In *Proceedings of the HLT-NAACL 2003 Workshop on Text Meaning, Volume 9 (HLT-NAACL-TEXTMEANING'03)*, pages 38–45, 2003. DOI: 10.3115/1119239.1119245. 27

Silviu Cucerzan. Large-scale named entity disambiguation based on Wikipedia data. In *Proceedings of the 2007 Joint Conference on Empirical Methods in Natural Language Processing and Computational Natural Language Learning (EMNLP-CoNLL 2007)*, pages 708–716, 2007. 19

Silviu Cucerzan. TAC entity linking by performing full-document entity extraction and disambiguation. In *Proceedings of the Fourth Text Analysis Conference (TAC 2011)*, 2011. 19

Aron Culotta and Jeffrey S. Sorensen. Dependency tree kernels for relation extraction. In *Proceedings of the 42nd Annual Meeting of the Association for Computational Linguistics (ACL'04)*, pages 423–429, 2004. DOI: 10.3115/1218955.1219009. 21, 22

Aron Culotta, Andrew McCallum, and Jonathan Betz. Integrating probabilistic extraction models and data mining to discover relations and patterns in text. In *Proceedings of the 2006 Conference of the North American Chapter of the Association for Computational Linguistics on Human Language Technology (HLT-NAACL'06)*, 2006. DOI: 10.3115/1220835.1220873. 21

Hamish Cunningham, Diana Maynard, Kalina Bontcheva, and Valentin Tablan. GATE: an architecture for development of robust HLT applications. In *Recent Advanced in Language Processing*, pages 168–175, 2002. DOI: 10.3115/1073083.1073112. 14

Hamish Cunningham, Valentin Tablan, Angus Roberts, and Kalina Bontcheva. Getting more out of biomedical documents with GATE's full lifecycle open source text analytics. *PLOS Computational Biology*, 2013. DOI: 10.1371/journal.pcbi.1002854. 14

Ido Dagan, Oren Glickman, and Bernardo Magnini. The PASCAL recognising textual entailment challenge. In *Machine Learning Challenges, Evaluating Predictive Uncertainty, Visual Object Classification and Recognizing Textual Entailment, First PASCAL Machine Learning Challenges Workshop (MLCW 2005)*, pages 177–190, 2005. DOI: 10.1007/11736790_9. 27

Chenyun Dai, Dan Lin, Elisa Bertino, and Murat Kantarcioglu. An approach to evaluate data trustworthiness based on data provenance. In *Proceedings of the 5th VLDB Workshop on Secure Data Management (SDM 2008)*, pages 82–98, 2008. DOI: 10.1007/978-3-540-85259-9_6. 1

Daryl J. Daley and David G. Kendall. Epidemics and rumours. *Nature*, 204:1118, 1964. DOI: 10.1038/2041118a0. 87

Manlio De Domenico, Albert Solé-Ribalta, Emanuele Cozzo, Mikko Kivelä, Yamir Moreno, Mason A. Porter, Sergio Gómez, and Alex Arenas. Mathematical formulation of multilayer networks. *Physical Review X*, 3(4):041022, 2013. DOI: 10.1103/PhysRevX.3.041022. 108

Manlio De Domenico, Mason A. Porter, and Alex Arenas. MuxViz: A tool for multilayer analysis and visualization of networks. *Journal of Complex Networks*, pages 159–176, 2014a. DOI: 10.1093/comnet/cnu038. 108

Manlio De Domenico, Albert Solé-Ribalta, Sergio Gómez, and Alex Arenas. Navigability of interconnected networks under random failures. *Proceedings of the National Academy of Sciences*, 111(23):8351–8356, 2014b. DOI: 10.1073/pnas.1318469111. 110

Marie-Catherine de Marneffe, Anna N. Rafferty, and Christopher D. Manning. Finding contradictions in text. In *Proceedings of the Annual Meeting on Association for Computational Linguistics: Human Language Technologies (ACL-HLT'08)*, pages 1039–1047, June 2008. 27

Gianluca Demartini, Tereza Iofciu, and Arjen P. De Vries. Overview of the INEX 2009 Entity Ranking Track. In *Proceedings of the Focused Retrieval and Evaluation, and 8th International Conference on Initiative for the Evaluation of XML Retrieval (INEX'09)*, pages 254–264, 2010. DOI: 10.1007/978-3-642-14556-8_26. 16

Hongbo Deng, Michael R. Lyu, and Irwin King. A generalized co-HITS algorithm and its application to bipartite graphs. In *Proceedings of the 15th ACM SIGKDD International Conference on Knowledge Discovery and Data Mining (KDD'09)*, pages 239–248, 2009. DOI: 10.1145/1557019.1557051. 25

Mieso K. Denko and Tao Sun. Probabilistic trust management in pervasive computing. In *Proceedings of the Embedded and Ubiquitous Computing Workshops (EUC 2008)*, pages 610–615. IEEE Computer Society, 2008. DOI: 10.1109/EUC.2008.149. 70

Xin Dong, Laure Berti-Equille, Yifan Hu, and Divesh Srivastava. SOLOMON: Seeking the truth via copying detection. *Proceedings of the VLDB Endowment*, 3(2):1617–1620, 2010a. DOI: 10.14778/1920841.1921054. 4

Xin Dong, Evgeniy Gabrilovich, Geremy Heitz, Wilko Horn, Ni Lao, Kevin Murphy, Thomas Strohmann, Shaohua Sun, and Wei Zhang. Knowledge Vault: A Web-scale approach to probabilistic knowledge fusion. In *Proceedings of the 20th ACM SIGKDD International Conference on Knowledge Discovery and Data Mining (KDD'14)*, pages 601–610, 2014a. DOI: 10.1145/2623330.2623623. 24, 39, 41, 56, 57

Xin Luna Dong and Divesh Srivastava. Compact explanation of data fusion decisions. In *Proceedings of the 22nd International World Wide Web Conference (WWW 2013)*, pages 379–390, 2013. 37

Xin Luna Dong, Laure Berti-Equille, and Divesh Srivastava. Integrating conflicting data: The role of source dependence. *Proceedings of the VLDB Endowment*, 2(1):550–561, 2009a. DOI: 10.14778/1687627.1687690. 34, 35, 36, 41, 54, 57

Xin Luna Dong, Laure Berti-Equille, and Divesh Srivastava. Truth discovery and copying detection in a dynamic world. *Proceedings of the VLDB Endowment*, 2(1):562–573, 2009b. DOI: 10.14778/1687627.1687691. 7, 41, 54, 57, 58, 111

Xin Luna Dong, Laure Berti-Equille, Yifan Hu, and Divesh Srivastava. Global detection of complex copying relationships between sources. *Proceedings of the VLDB Endowment*, 3(1-2): 1358–1369, September 2010b. DOI: 10.14778/1920841.1921008. 4, 7, 41, 54, 57

Xin Luna Dong, Evgeniy Gabrilovich, Geremy Heitz, Wilko Horn, Kevin Murphy, Shaohua Sun, and Wei Zhang. From data fusion to knowledge fusion. In *Proceedings of the VLDB Endowment*, 2014b. DOI: 10.14778/2732951.2732962. 7, 62

Sergey N. Dorogovtsev, Alexander V. Goltsev, and Jose F.F. Mendes. Critical phenomena in complex networks. *Reviews of Modern Physics*, 80(4):1275–1335, 2008. DOI: 10.1103/RevModPhys.80.1275. 77

Pat Doyle, Julia I. Lane, Jules J.M. Theeuwes, and Laura V. Zayatz. *Confidentiality, disclosure, and data access: Theory and practical applications for statistical agencies*. Elsevier Science, 2001. 92

Daniel M. Dunlavy, Tamara G. Kolda, and W. Philip Kegelmeyer. Multilinear algebra for analyzing data with multiple linkages. *Graph Algorithms in the Language of Linear Algebra*, pages 85–114, 2011. DOI: 10.1137/1.9780898719918.ch7. 108

Ahmed K. Elmagarmid, Panagiotis G. Ipeirotis, and Vassilios S. Verykios. Duplicate record detection: A survey. *IEEE Trans. on Knowl. and Data Eng.*, 19(1):1–16, January 2007. ISSN 1041-4347. DOI: 10.1109/TKDE.2007.250581. 19

Paul Erdös and Alfréd Rényi. On random graphs. *Publ. Math. (Debrecen)*, 6:290–297, 1959. 79, 83

Oren Etzioni, Michele Banko, Stephen Soderland, and Daniel S. Weld. Open information extraction from the Web. *Commun. ACM*, 51(12):68–74, 2008. DOI: 10.1145/1409360.1409378. 11

Wenfei Fan and Floris Geerts. *Foundations of Data Quality Management.* Synthesis Lectures on Data Management. Morgan & Claypool Publishers, 2012. DOI: 10.2200/S00439ED1V01Y201207DTM030. 1

Emilio Ferrara, Pasquale De Meo, Giacomo Fiumara, and Robert Baumgartner. Web data extraction, applications and techniques: A survey. *Knowledge-Based Systems*, 70:301–323, 2014. DOI: 10.1016/j.knosys.2014.07.007. 111

David Ferrucci and Adam Lally. UIMA: An architectural approach to unstructured information processing in the corporate research environment. *Nat. Lang. Eng.*, 10(3-4):327–348, September 2004. DOI: 10.1017/S1351324904003523. 14

Jenny Rose Finkel, Trond Grenager, and Christopher Manning. Incorporating non-local information into information extraction systems by Gibbs sampling. In *Proceedings of the 43rd Annual Meeting on Association for Computational Linguistics (ACL'05)*, pages 363–370, 2005. DOI: 10.3115/1219840.1219885. 18

Radu Florian, Hany Hassan, Hongyan Jing, Nanda Kambhatla, Xiaqiang Luo, Nicolas Nicolov, and Salim Roukos. A statistical model for multilingual entity detection and tracking. In *Proceedings of the 2004 Conference of the North American Chapter of the Association for Computational Linguistics on Human Language Technology (HLT-NAACL'04)*, pages 1–8, May 2004. 18

Santo Fortunato. Community detection in graphs. *Physics Reports*, 486(3-5):75–174, 2010. DOI: 10.1016/j.physrep.2009.11.002. 99

Linton C. Freeman. A set of measures of centrality based upon betweenness. *Sociometry*, 40, 1977. DOI: 10.2307/3033543. 81

Adrien Friggeri, Lada Adamic, Dean Eckles, and Justin Cheng. Rumor cascades. In *Proceedings of the Eighth International AAAI Conference on Weblogs and Social Media*, 2014. 97, 98

Carol J. Fung, Jie Zhang, Issam Aib, and Raouf Boutaba. Dirichlet-based trust management for effective collaborative intrusion detection networks. *IEEE Transactions on Network and Service Management*, 8(2):79 –91, June 2011. DOI: 10.1109/TNSM.2011.050311.100028. 66

Alban Galland, Serge Abiteboul, Amélie Marian, and Pierre Senellart. Corroborating information from disagreeing views. In *Proceedings of the ACM International Conference on Web Search and Data Mining (WSDM 2010)*, pages 131–140, 2010. DOI: 10.1145/1718487.1718504. 7, 35, 36, 42, 47

Diego Gambetta. Can we trust trust? In *Trust: Making and Breaking Cooperative Relations*, pages 213–237. Basil Blackwell, 1988. 63

Saurabh Ganeriwal, Laura K. Balzano, and Mani B. Srivastava. Reputation-based framework for high integrity sensor networks. *ACM Trans. Sen. Netw.*, 4(3):15:1–15:37, June 2008. ISSN 1550-4859. DOI: 10.1145/1362542.1362546. 65, 69

Jing Gao, Qi Li, Bo Zhao, Wei Fan, and Jiawei Han. Truth discovery and crowdsourcing aggregation: A unified perspective (Ttutorial). Proceedings of the International Conference on Very Large Data Bases (VLDB 2015), 2015a. 41

Jing Gao, Qi Li, Bo Zhao, Wei Fan, and Jiawei Han. Truth discovery and crowdsourcing aggregation: A unified perspective. *Proceedings of the VLDB Endowment*, 8(12):2048–2059, 2015b. DOI: 10.14778/2824032.2824136. 7

François Goasdoué, Konstantinos Karanasos, Yannis Katsis, Julien Leblay, Ioana Manolescu, and Stamatis Zampetakis. Fact checking and analyzing the Web. In *Proceedings of the ACM International Conference on Management of Data (SIGMOD 2013)*, pages 997–1000, 2013. DOI: 10.1145/2463676.2463692. 7, 107

William Goffman and Vaun A. Newill. Generalization of epidemic theory. An application to the transmission of ideas. *Nature*, 204:225–228, 1964. DOI: 10.1038/204225a0. 87

Jennifer Golbeck. Computing and applying trust in Web-based social networks. PhD thesis, University of Maryland. College Park, MD, USA, 2005. 72

Jennifer Golbeck, Bijan Parsia, and James Hendler. Trust networks on the semantic Web. In *Proceedings of Cooperative Intelligent Agents*, 2003. DOI: 10.1007/978-3-540-45217-1_18. 69

Sergio Gómez, Alex Arenas, Javier Borge-Holthoefer, Sandro Meloni, and Yamir Moreno. Discrete-time Markov chain approach to contact-based disease spreading in complex networks. *Europhysics Letters*, 89:38009, 2010. DOI: 10.1209/0295-5075/89/38009. 88

Sergio Gómez, Albert Diaz-Guilera, Jesus Gomez-Gardeñes, Conrad J Perez-Vicente, Yamir Moreno, and Alex Arenas. Diffusion dynamics on multiplex networks. *Physical Review Letters*, 110(2):028701, 2013. DOI: 10.1103/PhysRevLett.110.028701. 110

Edgar González and Jordi Turmo. Unsupervised relation extraction by massive clustering. In *Proceedings of The Ninth IEEE International Conference on Data Mining (ICDM'09)*, pages 782–787, 2009. DOI: 10.1109/ICDM.2009.81. 23

Sandra González-Bailón, Javier Borge-Holthoefer, Alejandro Rivero, and Yamir Moreno. The dynamics of protest recruitment through an online network. *Scientific Reports*, 1:197, 2011. DOI: 10.1038/srep00197. 96

Sandra González-Bailón, Javier Borge-Holthoefer, and Yamir Moreno. Broadcasters and hidden influentials in online protest diffusion. *American Behavioral Scientist*, 2013. DOI: 10.1177/0002764213479371. 97

Kannan Govindan and Prasant Mohapatra. Trust computations and trust dynamics in mobile adhoc networks: A survey. *IEEE Communications Surveys and Tutorials*, 14(2):279–298, 2012. DOI: 10.1109/SURV.2011.042711.00083. 65, 70

Ralph Grishman and Beth Sundheim. Message Understanding Conference-6: A brief history. In *Proceedings of the 16th Conference on Computational Linguistics, Volume 1 (COLING'96)*, pages 466–471, 1996. DOI: 10.3115/992628.992709. 11

R. Guha, Ravi Kumar, Prabhakar Raghavan, and Andrew Tomkins. Propagation of trust and distrust. In *Proceedings of the 13th International Conference on World Wide Web (WWW'04)*, pages 403–412, 2004. DOI: 10.1145/988672.988727. 71, 72

Roger Guimerà and Marta Sales-Pardo. Missing and spurious interactions and the reconstruction of complex networks. *Proceedings of the National Academy of Sciences*, 106(52):22073–22078, 2009. DOI: 10.1073/pnas.0908366106. 111

Zhou GuoDong, Su Jian, Zhang Jie, and Zhang Min. Exploring various knowledge in relation extraction. In *Proceedings of the 43rd Annual Meeting on Association for Computational Linguistics (ACL'05)*, pages 427–434, 2005. DOI: 10.3115/1219840.1219893. 21

Zoltán Gyöngyi, Hector Garcia-Molina, and Jan Pedersen. Combating Web spam with TrustRank. In *Proceedings of the Thirtieth International Conference on Very Large Data Bases, Volume 30 (VLDB'04)*, pages 576–587, 2004. 69

Aaron Halfaker, Aniket Kittur, Robert Kraut, and John Riedl. A jury of your peers: quality, experience and ownership in Wikipedia. In *Proceedings of the International Symposium on Wikis*, 2009. DOI: 10.1145/1641309.1641332. 103

Olaf Hartig. Provenance information in the Web of Data. In *Proceedings of the WWW2009 Workshop on Linked Data on the Web (LDOW 2009)*, 2009. DOI: 10.1007/978-3-642-17819-1_10. 2

Naeemul Hassan, Chengkai Li, and Mark Tremayne. Detecting check-worthy factual claims in presidential debates. In *Proceedings of the 24th ACM International on Conference on Information and Knowledge Management (CIKM'15)*, pages 1835–1838, 2015. DOI: 10.1145/2806416.2806652. 63

Herbert W. Hethcote. The mathematics of infectious diseases. *SIAM review*, 42(4):599–653, 2000. DOI: 10.1137/S0036144500371907. 87

Petter Holme and Jari Saramäki. Temporal networks. *Physics Reports*, 519(3):97–125, 2012. DOI: 10.1016/j.physrep.2012.03.001. 112

Hongzhao Huang, Yunbo Cao, Xiaojiang Huang, Heng Ji, and Chin-Yew Lin. Collective tweet Wikification based on semi-supervised graph regularization. In *Proceedings of the 52nd Annual Meeting of the Association for Computational Linguistics, Volume 1 (ACL'14)*, pages 380–390, June 2014. 19

Gerardo Iñiguez, Tzipe Govezensky, Robin Dunbar, Kimmo Kaski, and Rafael A. Barrio. Effects of deception in social networks. *Proceedings of the Royal Society of London B: Biological Sciences*, 281(1790):20141195, 2014. DOI: 10.1098/rspb.2014.1195. 97, 98

Arie Jacobi and Ofir Ben-Assuli. Distortion of a message propagated in a social network. In *Systems (ILAIS) Conference June 29, 2011 The Open University of Israel*, page 31, 2011. 92

Heng Ji. Challenges from information extraction to information fusion. In *Proceedings of the conference on Computational Linguistics (COLING'10)*, pages 507–515, 2010. 107

Heng Ji and Ralph Grishman. Knowledge base population: Successful approaches and challenges. In *Proceedings of the 49th Annual Meeting of the Association for Computational Linguistics: Human Language Technologies (ACL-HLT 2011)*, pages 1148–1158, 2011. 16, 19, 20

Heng Ji, Joel Nothman, and Ben Hachey. Overview of TAC-KBP2014 entity discovery and linking tasks. In *Proceedings of the Text Analysis Conference (TAC'14)*, November 2014. 19

Li Jia, Hongzhi Wang, Jianzhong Li, and Hong Gao. Incremental truth discovery for information from multiple data sources. In *Proceedings of the Web-Age Information Management (WAIM) 2013 International Workshops*, pages 56–66, 2013. DOI: 10.1007/978-3-642-39527-7_8. 7, 58

Yu Jiang, Guoliang Li, Jianhua Feng, and Wen-Syan Li. String similarity joins: An experimental evaluation. *Proceedings of the VLDB Endowment*, 7(8):625–636, 2014. DOI: 10.14778/2732296.2732299. 19

Audun Jøsang and Jochen Haller. Dirichlet reputation systems. In *Proceedings of the The Second International Conference on Availability, Reliability and Security (ARES'07)*, pages 112–119, 2007. DOI: 10.1109/ARES.2007.71. 64

Audun Jøsang and Roslan Ismail. The Beta reputation system. In *Proceedings of the 15th Bled Conference on Electronic Commerce*, 2002. 66

Audun Jøsang and Simon Pope. Semantic constraints for trust transitivity. In *Proceedings of the 2nd Asia-Pacific Conference on Conceptual Modelling, Volume 43 (APCCM'05)*, pages 59–68, 2005. 69

Audun Jøsang, Roslan Ismail, and Colin Boyd. A survey of trust and reputation systems for online service provision. *Decis. Support Syst.*, 43(2):618–644, March 2007. DOI: 10.1016/j.dss.2005.05.019. 65, 66

Nanda Kambhatla. Combining lexical, syntactic, and semantic features with maximum entropy models for extracting relations. In *Proceedings of the ACL 2004 on Interactive Poster and Demonstration Sessions (ACLdemo'04)*, 2004. DOI: 10.3115/1219044.1219066. 21

David Kempe, Jon Kleinberg, and Amit Kumar. Connectivity and inference problems for temporal networks. In *Proceedings of the 32nd ACM symposium on Theory of Computing*, pages 504–513, 2000. DOI: 10.1006/jcss.2002.1829. 112

David Kempe, Jon Kleinberg, and Éva Tardos. Maximizing the spread of influence through a social network. In *Proceedings of the 9th ACM SIGKDD international conference on Knowledge Discovery and Data Mining (KDD 2003)*, pages 137–146, 2003. DOI: 10.1145/956750.956769. 95

Maksim Kitsak, Lazaros K. Gallos, Shlomo Havlin, Fredrik Liljeros, Lev Muchnik, H. Eugene Stanley, and H.A. Makse. Identification of influential spreaders in complex networks. *Nature Physics*, 6(11):888–893, 2010. DOI: 10.1038/nphys1746. 8, 96

Mikko Kivelä, Alex Arenas, Marc Barthelemy, James P. Gleeson, Yamir Moreno, and Mason A. Porter. Multilayer networks. *Journal of Complex Networks*, 2(3):203–271, 2014. DOI: 10.1093/comnet/cnu016. 108

Jon M. Kleinberg. Hubs, authorities, and communities. *ACM Comput. Surv.*, 31(4es), December 1999. DOI: 10.1145/345966.345982. 41

Konstantin Klemm, M. Ángeles Serrano, Víctor M. Eguiluz, and Maxi San Miguel. A measure of individual role in collective dynamics: spreading at criticality. *Scientific Reports*, 2:292, 2012. DOI: 10.1038/srep00292. 96

Peter Klimek and Stefan Thurner. Triadic closure dynamics drives scaling laws in social multiplex networks. *New Journal of Physics*, 15(6):063008, 2013. DOI: 10.1088/1367-2630/15/6/063008. 110

Peter Klügl, Martin Toepfer, Florian Lemmerich, Andreas Hotho, and Frank Puppe. Collective information extraction with context-specific consistencies. In *Proceedings of the European Conference on Machine Learning and Knowledge Discovery in Databases (ECML/PKDD 2012)*, volume 7523 of *Lecture Notes in Computer Science*, pages 728–743. Springer, 2012. DOI: 10.1007/978-3-642-33460-3_52. 105

Tamara G. Kolda and Brett W. Bader. Tensor decompositions and applications. *SIAM Review*, 51(3):455–500, 2009. DOI: 10.1137/07070111X. 108

Natalia Konstantinova. Review of relation extraction methods: What is new out there? In *Proceedings of Third Analysis of Images, Social Networks and Texts International Conference (AIST 2004)*, pages 15–28, 2014. DOI: 10.1007/978-3-319-12580-0_2. 21

Sejeong Kwon, Meeyoung Cha, Kyomin Jung, Wei Chen, and Yajun Wang. Prominent features of rumor propagation in online social media. In *Proceedings of the IEEE International Conference on Data Mining (ICDM 2013)*, pages 1103 – 1108, 2013. DOI: 10.1109/ICDM.2013.61. 63

John D. Lafferty, Andrew McCallum, and Fernando C. N. Pereira. Conditional Random Fields: Probabilistic models for segmenting and labeling sequence data. In *Proceedings of the Eighteenth International Conference on Machine Learning (ICML 2001)*, pages 282–289, 2001. 105

Seungyoon Lee and Peter Monge. The coevolution of multiplex communication networks in organizational communities. *Journal of Communication*, 61(4):758–779, 2011. DOI: 10.1111/j.1460-2466.2011.01566.x. 110

Jure Leskovec, Mary McGlohon, Christos Faloutsos, Natalie Glance, and Matthew Hurst. Cascading behavior in large blog graphs. In *Proceedings of the 7th SIAM international conference on Data Mining (SDM 2007)*, pages 29406–13, 2007. DOI: 10.1137/1.9781611972771.60. 89

Jure Leskovec, Lars Backstrom, and Jon Kleinberg. Meme-tracking and the dynamics of the news cycle. In *Proceedings of the 15th ACM SIGKDD international conference on Knowledge Discovery and Data Mining (KDD 2009)*, pages 497–506, 2009. DOI: 10.1145/1557019.1557077. 9, 101, 102

R. Levien. Attack resistant trust metrics. PhD Thesis UC Berkeley LA, 2004. 41

Qi Li, Yaliang Li, Jing Gao, Lu Su, Bo Zhao, Murat Demirbas, Wei Fan, and Jiawei Han. A confidence-aware approach for truth discovery on long-tail data. *Proceedings of the VLDB Endowment*, 8(4):425–436, 2014. DOI: 10.14778/2735496.2735505. 7, 60, 103

Xian Li, Xin Luna Dong, Kenneth Lyons, Weiyi Meng, and Divesh Srivastava. Truth finding on the deep Web: Is the problem solved? *Proceedings of the VLDB Endowment*, 6(2):97–108, 2012. DOI: 10.14778/2535568.2448943. 7

Xian Li, Xin Luna Dong, Kenneth B. Lyons, Weiyi Meng, and Divesh Srivastava. Scaling up copy detection. In *Proceedings of the 31st IEEE International Conference on Data Engineering, (ICDE 2015)*, pages 89–100, 2015a. 38, 56, 62

Yaliang Li, Qi Li, Jing Gao, Lu Su, Bo Zhao, Wei Fan, and Jiawei Han. On the discovery of evolving truth. In *Proceedings of the 21th ACM SIGKDD International Conference on Knowledge Discovery and Data Mining (KDD'15)*, pages 675–684, 2015b. DOI: 10.1145/2783258.2783277. 7, 58, 111

Lucian Vlad Lita, Abe Ittycheriah, Salim Roukos, and Nanda Kambhatla. tRuEcasIng. In *Proceedings of the 41st Annual Meeting on Association for Computational Linguistics, Volume 1 (ACL'03)*, pages 152–159, 2003. DOI: 10.3115/1075096.1075116. 15

Xiaohua Liu, Yitong Li, Haocheng Wu, Ming Zhou, Furu Wei, and Yi Lu. Entity linking for tweets. In *Proceedings of the 51rst Annual Meeting of the Association for Computational Linguistics, Volume 1*, pages 1304–1311, 2013. 19

Huma Lodhi, Craig Saunders, John Shawe-Taylor, Nello Cristianini, and Chris Watkins. Text classification using string kernels. *J. Mach. Learn. Res.*, 2:419–444, March 2002. DOI: 10.1162/153244302760200687. 21

Andrey Y. Lokhov, Marc Mézard, Hiroki Ohta, and Lenka Zdeborová. Inferring the origin of an epidemic with dynamic message-passing algorithm. *Physical Review E*, 90(1):012801, 2014. DOI: 10.1103/PhysRevE.90.012801. 94

Edward Loper and Steven Bird. NLTK: The natural language toolkit. In *Proceedings of the ACL'02 Workshop on Effective Tools and Methodologies for Teaching Natural Language Processing and Computational Linguistics, Volume 1*, pages 63–70, 2002. DOI: 10.3115/1118108.1118117. 14, 16

Linyuan Lü and Tao Zhou. Link prediction in complex networks: A survey. *Physica A: Statistical Mechanics and its Applications*, 390(6):1150–1170, 2011. DOI: 10.1016/j.physa.2010.11.027. 111

Xiaoqiang Luo, Abe Ittycheriah, Hongyan Jing, Nanda Kambhatla, and Salim Roukos. A mention-synchronous coreference resolution algorithm based on the Bell tree. In *Proceedings of the 42nd Annual Meeting on Association for Computational Linguistics (ACL'04)*, 2004. DOI: 10.3115/1218955.1218973. 17, 18

Fenglong Ma, Yaliang Li, Qi Li, Minghui Qiu, Jing Gao, Shi Zhi, Lu Su, Bo Zhao, Heng Ji, and Jiawei Han. FaitCrowd: Fine grained truth discovery for crowdsourced data aggregation. In *Proceedings of the 21th ACM SIGKDD International Conference on Knowledge Discovery and Data Mining (KDD'15)*, pages 745–754, 2015. DOI: 10.1145/2783258.2783314. 7, 34, 60, 61

X.J. Ma, Wei Wang, Ying-Cheng Lai, and Zhigang Zheng. Information explosion on complex networks and control. *The European Physical Journal B-Condensed Matter and Complex Systems*, 76(1):179–183, 2010. DOI: 10.1140/epjb/e2010-00208-1. 92, 93

Mónica Marrero, Julián Urbano, Sonia Sánchez-Cuadrado, Jorge Morato, and Juan Miguel Gómez Berbís. Named entity recognition: Fallacies, challenges and opportunities. *Computer Standards & Interfaces*, 35(5):482–489, 2013. DOI: 10.1016/j.csi.2012.09.004. 16

Andrew McCallum and Ben Wellner. Conditional models of identity uncertainty with application to noun coreference. In *Proceedings of the Eighteenth Annual Conference on Neural Information Processing Systems*, pages 905–912, 2004. 17, 18

Rada Mihalcea and Andras Csomai. Wikify!: Linking documents to encyclopaedic knowledge. In *Proceedings of the Sixteenth ACM Conference on Information and Knowledge Management (CIKM 2007)*, pages 233–242, 2007. DOI: 10.1145/1321440.1321475. 19, 20

Rada Mihalcea and Paul Tarau. TextRank: Bringing order into text. In *Proceedings of the 2004 Conference on Empirical Methods in Natural Language Processing (EMNLP 2004)*, pages 404–411, 2004. 25

Stanley Milgram. The small world problem. *Psychology Today*, 2, 1967. 83

David N. Milne and Ian H. Witten. Learning to link with Wikipedia. In *Proceedings of the 17th ACM Conference on Information and Knowledge Management, (CIKM 2008)*, pages 509–518, 2008. DOI: 10.1145/1458082.1458150. 19

Mike Mintz, Steven Bills, Rion Snow, and Dan Jurafsky. Distant supervision for relation extraction without labeled data. In *Proceedings of the Joint Conference of the 47th Annual Meeting of the ACL and the 4th International Joint Conference on Natural Language Processing, Volume 2 (ACL '09)*, pages 1003–1011, 2009. 22, 24

Mohammad Momani. Trust models in wireless sensor networks: A survey. *Communications in Computer and Information Science*, 89:37–46, 2010. DOI: 10.1007/978-3-642-14478-3_4. 65

Yamir Moreno, Maziar Nekovee, and Amalio F. Pacheco. Dynamics of rumor spreading in complex networks. *Physical Review E*, 69(6):066130, 2004. DOI: 10.1103/PhysRevE.69.066130. 90, 91

Peter J. Mucha, Thomas Richardson, Kevin Macon, Mason A. Porter, and Jukka-Pekka Onnela. Community structure in time-dependent, multiscale, and multiplex networks. *Science*, 328 (5980):876–878, 2010. DOI: 10.1126/science.1184819. 110

Lik Mui, Mojdeh Mohtashemi, Cheewee Ang, Peter Szolovits, and Ari Halberstadt. Ratings in distributed systems: A bayesian approach. In *Proceedings of the 11th Workshop on Information Technologies and Systems*, 2001. 64

Koji Murakami, Eric Nichols, Suguru Matsuyoshi, Asuka Sumida, Shouko Masuda, Kentaro Inui, and Yuji Matumoto. Statement Map: Assisting information crediblity analysis by visualizing arguments. In *Proceedings of the 3rd Workshop on Information Credibility on the Web (WICOW'09)*, pages 43–50, 2009. DOI: 10.1145/1526993.1527004. 28

James D. Murray. *Mathematical Biology*. Springer-Verlag, Berlin, 1993. DOI: 10.1007/b98868. 87

David Nadeau and Satoshi Sekine. A survey of named entity recognition and classification. *Linguisticae Investigationes*, 30(1):3–26, January 2007. DOI: 10.1075/li.30.1.03nad. 16

Maziar Nekovee, Yamir Moreno, Ginestra Bianconi, and Matteo Marsili. Theory of rumour spreading in complex social networks. *Physica A: Statistical Mechanics and its Applications*, 374 (1):457–470, 2007. DOI: 10.1016/j.physa.2006.07.017. 89, 90

Mark Newman, A. Lazlo Barabási, and Duncan J. Watts. *The structure and dynamics of networks*. Princeton University Press, 2006. 77

Vincent Ng. Learning noun phrase anaphoricity to improve coreference resolution: Issues in representation and optimization. In *Proceedings of the 42nd Annual Meeting on Association for Computational Linguistics (ACL'04)*, 2004. DOI: 10.3115/1218955.1218975. 17

Vincent Ng and Claire Cardie. Improving machine learning approaches to coreference resolution. In *Proceedings of the 40th Annual Meeting on Association for Computational Linguistics (ACL'02)*, pages 104–111, 2002. DOI: 10.3115/1073083.1073102. 17, 18

Nam P. Nguyen, Guanhua Yan, My T. Thai, and Stephan Eidenbenz. Containment of misinformation spread in online social networks. In *Proceedings of the 3rd Annual ACM Web Science Conference*, pages 213–222, 2012. DOI: 10.1145/2380718.2380746. 98, 99

Feng Niu, Ce Zhang, Christopher Ré, and Jude Shavlik. Elementary: Large-scale knowledge-base construction via machine learning and statistical inference. *Int. J. Semant. Web Inf. Syst.*, 8(3):42–73, July 2012. DOI: 10.4018/jswis.2012070103. 24

Robin Wentao Ouyang, Lance Kaplan, Paul Martin, Alice Toniolo, Mani Srivastava, and Timothy J. Norman. Debiasing crowdsourced quantitative characteristics in local businesses and services. In *Proceedings of the 14th International Conference on Information Processing in Sensor Networks (IPSN'15)*, pages 190–201, 2015. DOI: 10.1145/2737095.2737116. 60, 61

Lawrence Page, Sergey Brin, Rajeev Motwani, and Terry Winograd. The PageRank citation ranking: Bringing order to the Web. Technical report, Stanford Digital Library Technologies Project, Standford, CA, 1998. 82

Chris D. Paice. Another stemmer. *SIGIR Forum*, 24(3):56–61, November 1990. ISSN 0163-5840. URL http://doi.acm.org/10.1145/101306.101310. DOI: 10.1145/101306.101310. 15

Aditya Pal, F. Maxwell Harper, and Joseph A. Konstan. Exploring question selection bias to identify experts and potential experts in community question answering. *ACM Transactions on Information Systems*, 30(2):10:1–10:28, May 2012. ISSN 1046-8188. DOI: 10.1145/2180868.2180872. 106

132 BIBLIOGRAPHY

Jeff Pasternack and Dan Roth. Knowing what to believe (when you already know something). In *Proceedings of the Conference on Computational Linguistics (COLING'10)*, pages 877–885, 2010. 42

Jeff Pasternack and Dan Roth. Latent credibility analysis. In *Proceedings of the International World Wide Web Conference (WWW 2013)*, pages 1009–1020, 2013. 7, 36, 39, 47, 49, 50

Romualdo Pastor-Satorras and Alessandro Vespignani. Epidemic spreading in scale-free networks. *Physical Review Letters*, 86(14):3200–3203, 2001. ISSN 1079-7114. DOI: 10.1103/PhysRevLett.86.3200. 8, 88

Nicola Perra, Andrea Baronchelli, Delia Mocanu, Bruno Gonçalves, Romualdo Pastor-Satorras, and Alessandro Vespignani. Random walks and search in time-varying networks. *Physical Review Letters*, 109(23):238701, 2012. DOI: 10.1103/PhysRevLett.109.238701. 113

Enoch Peserico and Luca Pretto. Score and rank convergence of HITS. In *Proceedings of the 32nd Annual International ACM SIGIR Conference on Research and Development in Information Retrieval*, pages 770–771, 2009. DOI: 10.1145/1571941.1572120. 26

Pedro C. Pinto, Patrick Thiran, and Martin Vetterli. Locating the source of diffusion in large-scale networks. *Physical Review Letters*, 109(6):068702, 2012. DOI: 10.1103/PhysRevLett.109.068702. 94, 95

Ravali Pochampally, Anish Das Sarma, Xin Luna Dong, Alexandra Meliou, and Divesh Srivastava. Fusing data with correlations. In *Proceedings of the 2014 ACM SIGMOD International Conference on Management of Data (SIGMOD 2014)*, pages 433–444, 2014. DOI: 10.1145/2588555.2593674. 7, 36, 38, 41

M. F. Porter. *Readings in Information Retrieval*, chapter An Algorithm for Suffix Stripping, pages 313–316. Morgan Kaufmann Publishers Inc., San Francisco, CA, USA, 1997. ISBN 1-55860-454-5. 15

Altaf Rahman and Vincent Ng. Supervised models for coreference resolution. In *Proceedings of the 2009 Conference on Empirical Methods in Natural Language Processing, Volume 2 (EMNLP'09)*, pages 968–977, 2009. DOI: 10.3115/1699571.1699639. 18

Sarvapali D. Ramchurn, Dong Huynh, and Nicholas R. Jennings. Trust in multi-agent systems. *Knowl. Eng. Rev.*, 19(1):1–25, March 2004. DOI: 10.1017/S0269888904000116. 65

Anatol Rapoport. Spread of information through a population with socio-structural bias I. Assumption of transitivity. *The Bulletin of Mathematical Biophysics*, 15:523–533, 1953. DOI: 10.1007/BF02476441. 87

Lev-Arie Ratinov and Dan Roth. Design challenges and misconceptions in named entity recognition. In *Proceedings of the Thirteenth Conference on Computational Natural Language Learning (CoNLL 2009)*, pages 147–155, 2009. DOI: 10.3115/1596374.1596399. 16

Lev-Arie Ratinov and Dan Roth. Learning-based multi-sieve co-reference resolution with knowledge. In *Proceedings of the 2012 Joint Conference on Empirical Methods in Natural Language Processing and Computational Natural Language Learning (EMNLP-CoNLL 2012)*, pages 1234–1244, 2012. 20

Jacob Ratkiewicz, Michael Conover, Mark Meiss, Bruno Gonçalves, Snehal Patil, Alessandro Flammini, and Filippo Menczer. Truthy: Mapping the spread of astroturf in microblog streams. In *Proceedings of the 20th international conference companion on World Wide Web (WWW 2011)*, pages 249–252, 2011. DOI: 10.1145/1963192.1963301. 98

Ronald C. Read and Robin J. Wilson. *An atlas of graphs.* Oxford University Press, 1998. 82

Theodoros Rekatsinas, Xin Luna Dong, and Divesh Srivastava. Characterizing and selecting fresh data sources. In *Proceedings of the ACM SIGMOD International Conference on Management of Data (SIGMOD 2014)*, pages 919–930, 2014. DOI: 10.1145/2588555.2610504. 1

Paul Resnick, Ko Kuwabara, Richard Zeckhauser, and Eric Friedman. Reputation systems. *Commun. ACM*, 43(12):45–48, December 2000. DOI: 10.1145/355112.355122. 70

Lev Reyzin and Robert E. Schapire. How boosting the margin can also boost classifier complexity. In *Proceedings of the Twenty-Third International Conference on Machine Learning (ICML 2006)*, pages 753–760, 2006. DOI: 10.1145/1143844.1143939. 24

Bruno Ribeiro, Nicola Perra, and Andrea Baronchelli. Quantifying the effect of temporal resolution on time-varying networks. *Scientific Reports*, 3, 2013. DOI: 10.1038/srep03006. 113

Sebastian Riedel, Limin Yao, Andrew McCallum, and Benjamin M. Marlin. Relation extraction with matrix factorization and universal schemas. In *Proceedings of Human Language Technologies: Conference of the North American Chapter of the Association of Computational Linguistics (HLT-NAACL 2013)*, pages 74–84, 2013. 24

Alan Ritter, Doug Downey, Stephen Soderland, and Oren Etzioni. It's a contradiction—no, it's not: A case study using functional relations. In *Proceedings of the Conference on Empirical Methods in Natural Language Processing (EMNLP'08)*, pages 11–20, 2008. DOI: 10.3115/1613715.1613718. 27

Angus Roberts, Robert J. Gaizauskas, Mark Hepple, and Yikun Guo. Combining terminology resources and statistical methods for entity recognition: an evaluation. In *Proceedings of the International Conference on Language Resources and Evaluation, (LREC'08)*, 2008. 16

Benjamin Roth, Emma Strubell, John Sullivan, Lakshmi Vikraman, Katherine Silverstein, and Andrew McCallum. Universal Schema for Slot-Filling, Cold-Start KBP and Event Argument Extraction: UMassIESL at TAC KBP 2014. In *Proceedings of the Text Analysis Conference (Knowledge Base Population Track) Workshop (TAC KBP 2014)*, November 2014. 24

John I. Saeed. *Semantics*. Wiley-Blackwell Publishing, 2009. 105

Barna Saha and Divesh Srivastava. Data quality: The other face of Big Data (tutorial). In *Proceedings of the IEEE International Conference on Data Engineering (ICDE 2014)*, pages 1294–1297, 2014. DOI: 10.1109/ICDE.2014.6816764. 2

Mariam Salloum, Xin Luna Dong, Divesh Srivastava, and Vassilis J. Tsotras. Online ordering of overlapping data sources. *Proceedings of the VLDB Endowment*, 7(3):133–144, 2013. DOI: 10.14778/2732232.2732233. 1

Mark Sammons, Yangqiu Song, Ruichen Wang, Gourab Kundu, Chen-Tse Tsai, Shyam Upadhyay, Siddarth Ancha, Stephen Mayhew, and Dan Roth. Overview of UI-CCG systems for event argument extraction, entity discovery and linking, and slot filler validation. In *Proceedings of the Seventh Text Analysis Conference (TAC 2014)*, 2014. 24

Joaquín Sanz, Cheng-Yi Xia, Sandro Meloni, and Yamir Moreno. Dynamics of interacting diseases. *Physical Review X*, 4(4):041005, 2014. DOI: 10.1103/PhysRevX.4.041005. 111

Satoshi Sekine. Extended named entity ontology with attribute information. In *Proceedings of the International Conference on Language Resources and Evaluation, LREC'08*, 2008. 17

Wei Shen, Jianyong Wang, Ping Luo, and Min Wang. Linking named entities in tweets with knowledge base via user interest modeling. In *Proceedings of the 19th ACM SIGKDD International Conference on Knowledge Discovery and Data Mining (KDD'13)*, pages 68–76, 2013. DOI: 10.1145/2487575.2487686. 19

Wei Shen, Jianyong Wang, and Jiawei Han. Entity linking with a knowledge base: Issues, techniques, and solutions. *IEEE Trans. Knowl. Data Eng.*, 27(2):443–460, 2015. DOI: 10.1109/TKDE.2014.2327028. 19

Georgios Sigletos, Georgios Paliouras, Constantine D. Spyropoulos, and Michael Hatzopoulos. Combining information extraction systems using voting and stacked generalization. *Journal of Machine Learning Research*, 6:1751–1782, 2005. 24

Matthew P. Simmons, Lada Adamic, and Eytan Adar. Memes online: Extracted, subtracted, injected, and recollected. *Proceedings of the 5th AAAI Conference on Web and Social Media*, 11: 17–21, 2011. 102

Parag Singla and Pedro Domingos. Multi-relational record linkage. In *Proceedings of the KDD-2004 Workshop on Multi-Relational Data Mining*, pages 31–48, 2004. 17

Wee Meng Soon, Hwee Tou Ng, and Daniel Chung Yong Lim. A machine learning approach to coreference resolution of noun phrases. *Comput. Linguist.*, 27(4):521–544, December 2001. DOI: 10.1162/089120101753342653. 17, 18

Valentin I. Spitkovsky and Angel X. Chang. A cross-lingual dictionary for English Wikipedia concepts. In *Proceedings of the Eight International Conference on Language Resources and Evaluation (LREC'12)*, May 2012. 15

Michele Starnini, Andrea Baronchelli, Alain Barrat, and Romualdo Pastor-Satorras. Random walks on temporal networks. *Physical Review E*, 85(5):056115, 2012. DOI: 10.1103/PhysRevE.85.056115. 113

Stephanie Strassel, Mark Przybocki, Kay Peterson, Zhiyi Song, and Kazuaki Maeda. Linguistic resources and evaluation techniques for evaluation of cross-document automatic content extraction. In *Proceedings of the Sixth International Conference on Language Resources and Evaluation (LREC'08)*, May 2008. 16

Jimeng Sun, Dacheng Tao, and Christos Faloutsos. Beyond streams and graphs: dynamic tensor analysis. In *Proceedings of the 12th ACM SIGKDD International Conference on Knowledge Discovery and Data Mining (KDD 2006)*, pages 374–383, 2006a. DOI: 10.1145/1150402.1150445. 108

Yan Lindsay Sun, Wei Yu, Zhu Han, and K. J.R. Liu. Information theoretic framework of trust modeling and evaluation for ad hoc networks. *IEEE J.Sel. A. Commun.*, 24(2):305–317, September 2006b. DOI: 10.1109/JSAC.2005.861389. 69

Yizhou Sun and Jiawei Han. Mining heterogeneous information networks: A structural analysis approach. *ACM SIGKDD Explorations Newsletter*, 14(2):20–28, 2013. DOI: 10.1145/2481244.2481248. 108

Mihai Surdeanu, Julie Tibshirani, Ramesh Nallapati, and Christopher D. Manning. Multi-instance multi-label learning for relation extraction. In *Proceedings of the 2012 Joint Conference on Empirical Methods in Natural Language Processing and Computational Natural Language Learning (EMNLP-CoNLL'12)*, pages 455–465, 2012. 22

Krishnaprasad Thirunarayan, Pramod Anantharam, Cory A. Henson, and Amit P. Sheth. Comparative trust management with applications: Bayesian approaches emphasis. *Future Generation Comp. Syst.*, 31:182–199, 2014. DOI: 10.1016/j.future.2013.05.006. 7, 65, 66

Erik F. Tjong Kim Sang and Fien De Meulder. Introduction to the CoNLL-2003 shared task: Language-independent named entity recognition. In *Proceedings of the 2003 Conference of the North American Chapter of the Association for Computational Linguistics on Human Language Technology, Volume 4 (CONLL'03)*, pages 142–147, 2003. DOI: 10.3115/1119176.1119195. 16

Kristina Toutanova, Dan Klein, Christopher D. Manning, and Yoram Singer. Feature-rich part-of-speech tagging with a cyclic dependency network. In *Proceedings of the 2003 Conference of the North American Chapter of the Association for Computational Linguistics on Human Language Technology, Volume 1 (HLT-NAACL'03)*, pages 173–180, 2003. DOI: 10.3115/1073445.1073478. 15

Jeffrey Travers and Stanley Milgram. An experimental study of the small world problem. *Sociometry*, 32(4):425–443, 1969. DOI: 10.2307/2786545. 83

Alessandro Vespignani. Modelling dynamical processes in complex socio-technical systems. *Nature Physics*, 8(1):32–39, 2012. DOI: 10.1038/nphys2160. 112

Vidhoon Viswanathan, Nazneen Fatema Rajani, Yinon Bentor, and Raymond J. Mooney. Stacked ensembles of information extractors for knowledge-base population. In *Proceedings of the 53rd Annual Meeting of the Association for Computational Linguistics and the 7th International Joint Conference on Natural Language Processing of the Asian Federation of Natural Language Processing, Volume 1 (ACL'15)*, pages 177–187, 2015. DOI: 10.3115/v1/P15-1018. 25

Ding-Jung Han Vittorio Castelli, Radu Florian. Slot filling through statistical processing and inference rules. In *Proceedings of the TAC 2010 Knowledge Base Population Track*, 2010. 18

Jan Vosecky, Dan Hong, and Vincent Y. Shen. User identification across multiple social networks. In *Proceedings of the 1st international conference on Networked Digital Technologies*, pages 360–365, 2009. DOI: 10.1109/NDT.2009.5272173. 111

V. G. Vinod Vydiswaran, ChengXiang Zhai, Dan Roth, and Peter Pirolli. Overcoming bias to learn about controversial topics. *Journal of the American Society for Information Science and Technology (JASIST)*, 66(8):1655–1672, 2014. DOI: 10.1002/asi.23274. 28

Dalia Attia Waguih and Laure Berti-Equille. Truth discovery algorithms: An experimental evaluation, qcri technical report, may 2014., 2014. 37, 61

Dalia Attia Waguih, Naman Goel, Hossam M. Hammady, and Laure Berti-Equille. Allegator-Track: Combining and reporting results of truth discovery from multi-source data. In *Proceedings of the IEEE International Conference on Data Engineering (ICDE 2015)*, pages 1440–1443, 2015. DOI: 10.1109/ICDE.2015.7113396. 37

Hanna M. Wallach. Topic modeling: Beyond bag-of-words. In *Proceedings of the International Conference on Machine Learning (ICML'06)*, 2006. DOI: 10.1145/1143844.1143967. 60

Chi Wang, Kaushik Chakrabarti, Tao Cheng, and Surajit Chaudhuri. Targeted disambiguation of ad-hoc, homogeneous sets of named entities. In *Proceedings of the 21st World Wide Web Conference (WWW 2012)*, pages 719–728, 2012a. DOI: 10.1145/2187836.2187934. 16

Dong Wang, Lance M. Kaplan, Hieu Khac Le, and Tarek F. Abdelzaher. On truth discovery in social sensing: A maximum likelihood estimation approach. In *Proceedings of the International Conference on Information Processing in Sensor Networks (IPSN 2012)*, pages 233–244, New York, USA, 2012b. DOI: 10.1145/2185677.2185737. 35, 47, 48

I-Jeng Wang, Edwina Liu, Cash Costello, and Christine D. Piatko. JHUAPL TAC-KBP2013 slot filler validation system. In *Proceedings of the Sixth Text Analysis Conference (TAC 2013)*, 2013. 24

Xianzhi Wang, Quan Z. Sheng, Xiu Susie Fang, Xue Li, Xiaofei Xu, and Lina Yao. Approximate truth discovery via problem scale reduction. In *Proceedings of the 24th ACM Conference on Information and Knowledge Management (CIKM 2015)*, October 2015a. DOI: 10.1145/2806416.2806444. 7, 35, 59, 62

Xianzhi Wang, Quan Z. Sheng, Xiu Susie Fang, Lina Yao, Xiaofei Xu, and Xue Li. An integrated bayesian approach for effective multi-truth discovery. In *Proceedings of the 24th ACM Conference on Information and Knowledge Management (CIKM 2015)*, October 2015b. DOI: 10.1145/2806416.2806443. 36, 39, 41, 59

Stanley Wasserman and Katherine Faust. *Social Network Analysis: Methods and Applications.* Cambridge University Press, Cambridge, 1994. 80

Duncan J. Watts. A simple model of global cascades on random networks. *Proceedings of the National Academy of Sciences*, 99(9):5766–5771, 2002. DOI: 10.1073/pnas.082090499. 110

Duncan J. Watts and Steven Strogatz. Collective dynamics of "small-world" networks. *Nature*, 393:440, 1998. DOI: 10.1038/30918. 79, 80, 84

Lilian Weng, Filippo Menczer, and Yong-Yeol Ahn. Virality prediction and community structure in social networks. *Scientific Reports*, 3, 2013. DOI: 10.1038/srep02522. 100

Michael Wick, Aron Culotta, Khashayar Rohanimanesh, and Andrew Mccallum. An entity based model for coreference resolution, 2009. DOI: 10.1137/1.9781611972795.32. 17

Yulan Yan, Naoaki Okazaki, Yutaka Matsuo, Zhenglu Yang, and Mitsuru Ishizuka. Unsupervised relation extraction by mining Wikipedia texts using information from the Web. In *Proceedings of the Joint Conference of the 47th Annual Meeting of the ACL and the 4th International Joint Conference on Natural Language Processing of the AFNLP, Volume 2 (ACL'09)*, pages 1021–1029, 2009. 23

Li Yang and Alma Cemerlic. Integrating dirichlet reputation into usage control. In *Proceedings of the 5th Annual Workshop on Cyber Security and Information Intelligence Research: Cyber Security and Information Intelligence Challenges and Strategies (CSIIRW'09)*, pages 62:1–62:4, 2009. DOI: 10.1145/1558607.1558679. 66

Xiaofeng Yang, Jian Su, Guodong Zhou, and Chew Lim Tan. An NP-cluster based approach to coreference resolution. In *Proceedings of the 20th International Conference on Computational Linguistics (COLING'04)*, 2004. DOI: 10.3115/1220355.1220388. 17

Xiaofeng Yang, Jian Su, Jun Lang, Chew Lim Tan, Ting Liu, and Sheng Li. An entity-mention model for coreference resolution with inductive logic programming. In *Proceedings of the 46th Annual Meeting on Association for Computational Linguistics (ACL'08)*, pages 843–851, 2008. 17

Xiaoxin Yin and Wenzhao Tan. Semi-supervised truth discovery. In *Proceedings of the International World Wide Web Conference (WWW 2011)*, pages 217–226, 2011. DOI: 10.1145/1963405.1963439. 26, 52, 54

Xiaoxin Yin, Jiawei Han, and Philip S. Yu. Truth discovery with multiple conflicting information providers on the Web. *IEEE Transactions on Knowledge and Data Engineering*, 20(6):796–808, 2008. DOI: 10.1109/TKDE.2007.190745. 35, 42, 45

Dian Yu, Hongzhao Huang, Taylor Cassidy, Heng Ji, Chi Wang, Shi Zhi, Jiawei Han, Clare R. Voss, and Malik Magdon-Ismail. The wisdom of minority: Unsupervised slot filling validation based on multi-dimensional truth-finding. In *Proceedings of the 25th International Conference on Computational Linguistics (COLING'14)*, pages 1567–1578, 2014. 25, 26

Dian Yu, Heng Ji, Sujian Li, and Chin-Yew Lin. Why read if you can scan? Trigger scoping strategy for biographical fact extraction. In *Proceedings of the 2015 Conference of the North American Chapter of the Association for Computational Linguistics on Human Language Technology (NAACL-HLT 2015)*, pages 1203–1208, 2015. DOI: 10.3115/v1/N15-1126. 25

Amrapali Zaveri, Andrea Maurino, and Laure Berti-Equille. Web data quality: Current state and new challenges. *Int. J. Semantic Web Inf. Syst.*, 10(2):1–6, 2014. DOI: 10.4018/ijswis.2014040101. 1

Dmitry Zelenko, Chinatsu Aone, and Anthony Richardella. Kernel methods for relation extraction. *J. Mach. Learn. Res.*, 3:1083–1106, March 2003. 21

Bo Zhao, Benjamin I. P. Rubinstein, Jim Gemmell, and Jiawei Han. A bayesian approach to discovering truth from conflicting sources for data integration. *Proceedings of the VLDB Endowment*, 5(6):550–561, 2012. DOI: 10.14778/2168651.2168656. 7, 34, 35, 36, 39, 47, 50, 52

Zhou Zhao, James Cheng, and Wilfred Ng. Truth discovery in data streams: A single-pass probabilistic approach. In *Proceedings of the 23rd ACM International Conference on Conference on Information and Knowledge Management (CIKM 2014)*, pages 1589–1598, 2014. DOI: 10.1145/2661829.2661892. 7, 58, 111

Shi Zhi, Bo Zhao, Wenzhu Tong, Jing Gao, Dian Yu, Heng Ji, and Jiawei Han. Modeling truth existence in truth discovery. In *Proceedings of the 21st ACM SIGKDD International Conference on Knowledge Discovery and Data Mining (KDD'15)*, pages 1543–1552, 2015. DOI: 10.1145/2783258.2783339. 7, 32, 37, 39, 59

Authors' Biographies

LAURE BERTI-ÉQUILLE

Dr. Laure Berti-Équille has been a Senior Scientist at Qatar Computing Research Institute (QCRI), Hamad Bin Khalifa University, since 2013. Prior to joining QCRI, Laure was a "Directeur de Recherche" at IRD, the French Institute of Research for Development (2011–2013), a tenured Associate Professor at University of Rennes 1 in France (2000–2010), and a visiting researcher at AT&T Labs-Research (NJ, USA) (2007–2009) when she received a Marie Curie fellowship of the European Commission (Grant FP6-MOIF-CT-2006-041000). Her research interests focus on developing novel data management and analytics techniques for truth discovery, anomaly detection, data fusion, and data curation. She has published one monograph, several book chapters, and over 80 research papers in refereed journals and conferences. She has served on the organization and program committees of over 50 international conferences and workshops. She is an associate editor of the *ACM Journal of Data and Information Quality* (JDIQ).

JAVIER BORGE-HOLTHOEFER

Dr. Javier Borge-Holthoefer, currently a Scientist at the Qatar Computing Research Institute (QCRI), Hamad bin Khalifa University, received a Ph.D. in Computer Science from the Universitat Rovira i Virgili (URV) in Tarragona (Catalonia, Spain) in 2011. Founded on interdisciplinary Physics, his research is focused on complex systems ranging from Cognitive Dynamics to Social Networks. Among other appointments, he taught at the Department of Computer Science and Mathematics and at the Department of Psychology (both in URV). Before moving to Qatar in 2014, he was a member of the COSNET Lab and held a position as a post-doctoral fellow at the Institute for Biocomputation and Physics of Complex Systems (BIFI), which belongs to the University of Zaragoza (Spain). With more than 20 peer-reviewed articles, his work has been published (among others) in the *EPJ Data Science, Physical Review E, PLoS One, Scientific Reports* and *Europhysics Letters*. Dr. Borge-Holthoefer has also contributed three chapters to different books around the problem of disease and information spreading on complex networks.